Spreading Happiness.Reimagining Tea.

BIRD & BLEND TEA CO.

BREW, BAKE, SIP & SAVOUR

BIRD & BLEND TEA CO.

BREW, BAKE, SIP & SAVOUR

60 recipes to make with tea

EBURY
PRESS

CONTENTS

Welcome to Our Magical World of Tea   6

Welcome to the Tea Wall   10

The Basics   18

Black   44

Green   60

Oolong   72

Herbal   84

Fruity   98

Rooibos   112

Matcha   130

Index   152

WELCOME TO OUR MAGICAL WORLD OF TEA

Hi, I'm Krisi, co-founder and owner of Bird & Blend Tea Co. I'm so excited to share with you our first-ever recipe book, full of carefully created and delicious tea-based recipes, from luscious drinks to decadent bakes and savoury bites.

When I first set about building Bird & Blend back in 2012, one of my passions was showcasing the diverse range of flavours and ways of experimenting with tea. I sat and sketched 'Spreading Happiness. Reimagining Tea' on the back of a napkin, and the rest is history!

As Chief Tea Mixologist (my alternative job title!), I am the visionary behind our incredible tea innovation and creative blends – I'm still creating many of them to this day. My goal is to ensure that every single tea we make tastes great, smells great and adds a bit of magic to our customers' days.

Over the years I have created loads of recipes with tea, and customers and team members have added their own too, so this book is an exciting collection of my favourites so far. There are soothing herbal infusions, like the

Deckchair Dreaming Cocktail (see page 90) and Enchanted Dreams Hot Chocolate (see page 86), and uplifting matcha-charged snacks like the Matcha Cookies (see page 137) and Matcha Protein Balls (see page 140). Oh, and don't forget the showstopping cakes!

I hope you are inspired to delve into these recipes and discover how magical the world of tea can be.

Krisi x

ABOUT US

Bird & Blend Tea Co. is an eco-conscious, independent, people-focused, award-winning tea company on a mission to spread happiness and reimagine tea. We're tea mixology experts and with over 100 blends, special seasonal teas and matcha on our famous Tea Wall, it's easy to see why our customers have described us as tea magicians! Tea is our TEAm's passion, so whether you're reading this book, browsing our website, chatting with us on social media or popping into the store, we're here to help you explore the magical world of tea.

Our start-up story

Co-founders Krisi and Mike set up the company at the age of 23 after returning from Canada, where they had been working as ski instructors and where the idea for Bird & Blend was born. From day one they put sustainability high on their priority list and this has not changed. They keep people and the planet at the forefront of decision-making, and Krisi and Mike went from packing tea in their back bedroom to having 200+ staff, 20 stores (and counting!) across the UK, plus a thriving international online store. Bird & Blend is leading the way in tea innovation in the UK.

Sustainability

Striving to be an eco-friendly tea company is a big part of why Bird & Blend Tea Co. exists and has always been part of the founders' decision-making. Our tea and packaging is 100% plastic free (and has been since day one) and either recyclable or home compostable. We are proud to be B Corp certified, which means we pledge to use our company as a force for good. People and planet have been and will remain at the heart of everything we do. We acknowledge that we aren't perfect and that sustainability isn't easy, it's an ever-evolving process and that's why every year we publish our improvement goals for our community.

What does B Corp certified mean?

A B Corp is an organisation that is certified as sustainable and ethical, which sees people and the planet as important as profit. B Corp certification looks at the entirety of a business's operations and covers five key areas: governance, workers, community, environment and customers.

The certification process is rigorous, with applicants required to reach a benchmark score of over 80, while providing evidence of socially and environmentally responsible practices relating to energy supplies, waste and water use, worker compensation, diversity and corporate transparency.

Certified

B Corporation

Join our communiTEA

Visit us in store for a delightful introduction to our iconic Tea Wall, enjoy one of our tea experience workshops or book us for a private tea experience. Visit us online where you can explore all of our tea blends and matcha flavours, join our Tea Tasting Club, and sign up to our newsletter, which ensures you get first look at our limited edition seasonal favourites – new and returning. You can also find out how to become one of our earth friendly tea wholesale partners and be as passionate about sustainability as we are. Discover our collaboration teas, tea-infused chocolate and teaware you won't be able to resist!

Pop in and visit us in person! We have stores across the UK. To find your local store, check out our store finder on our website.

WELCOME TO
THE TEA WALL

Our famous Tea Wall is the centrepiece of our
in-store experience, where you'll find over
100 delicious loose leaf tea blends using many
different tea types, flavours and
other colourful ingredients!

Here is a selection of magical tea blends
from the Tea Wall that we have used to create the
recipes inside this book...

Meet our Chocolate Digestives tea

A velvety smooth, caramel and chocolate black tea blend, best enjoyed while dunkin' the real thing!

You can find recipes using me on pages 35 and 52.
We love pairing this tea as a cuppa with a slice of Peppermint and Chocolate Cake (recipe page 75).

Meet our Earl Grey Creme tea

Fresh and fragrant with a hint of vanilla, our best-selling, award-winning Earl Grey blend has been part of our collection since day one.

You can find recipes using me on pages 33 and 48.
We love sipping this warming cuppa with anything sweet or savoury. It's yummy just on its own too!

Meet our Smoky Russian tea

Inspired by the ancient classic Russian caravan tea that got its smoky flavour from the evening campfires along the old tea trade routes. It's a pinewood-smoked Lapsang Souchong black tea, blended with Formosa Oolong, giving it a strong smoky flavour profile.

You can find recipes using me on pages 46 and 54.

Meet our Chinese Treasures tea

Inspired by eight treasures tea, we've created our own blend of this ancient elixir. Originating from Yunnan, China, this powerful blend is renowned for its medicinal and healing properties, with ginseng and spices to create the perfect warming brew.

Learn how to brew me so I don't burn on page 27.
You can find recipes using me on pages 63, 66 and 70.

Meet our MojiTEA tea

This is our bestselling green tea, inspired by the Mojito cocktail, a refreshing blend of peppermint and lime. It's full of flavour, is great hot but is fantastic cold, as an iced cold brew tea, or in a cocktail or mocktail.

Try our ultimate iced cocktail recipe on page 67.
We love to pair a MojiTEA cocktail with Iced Tea Doughnuts (page 103) for some fruity fun.

Meet our Ankara Apple tea

This is our tribute to Turkish apple tea and it uses an unusual but wonderfully moreish combination of green tea, apple pieces, cinnamon, cloves and pomegranate flowers. Evocative of busy buzzy days exploring markets and lazy afternoons sipping tea on the roadsides of Ankara.

You can find a recipe using me on page 68.

Meet our Peppermint Cream tea

This is a recreation of that perfect peppermint cream taste in a milk oolong tea blend. Naturally sweet, creamy notes are blended with soft mint and smooth cocoa. Yummy velvety chocolate goodness!

We've used this in our Peppermint and Chocolate Cake recipe on page 75.
You can find recipes using me on pages 79, 80 and 82.

Meet our Milk Oolong Chai tea

This creamy oolong with cocoa shells and chilli is mixed with the warming spices of chai including cardamom and cinnamon to create a truly unique cuppa with a dreamy aroma.

A naturally sweet tea treat that lasts and lasts - you can re-steep this blend up to seven times.
You can find recipes using me on pages 79, 80 and 82.

Meet our Enchanted Narnia tea

Inspired by the classic sweet, Turkish Delight, this is the most dreamy and smooth herbal tea, full of wonder. Visually beautiful with a chocolate rose aroma, get ready to be transported through the wardrobe to Narnia!

You can find recipes using me on pages 86, 92, 93 and 95. We love this blend cold brewed with lemonade: trust us, it's just as good as an iced tea as a dreamy hot cuppa.

Meet our Deckchair Dreaming tea

This is a calming chamomile blend, with hints of crisp apple, to be enjoyed relaxing on a deckchair at the beach or snoozing in the back garden. You'll be dreaming all year round!

You can find recipes using me on pages 88 and 90. We love this blend cold brewed in the summer paired with our Eton Mess recipe (page 89), so refreshing and relaxing.

Meet our Dozy Girl tea

Our ever-popular sleepy tea is a comforting combination of lavender, chamomile and rose; it's naturally caffeine-free and the perfect blend for getting cosy before bedtime. Our customers tell us it's 'a miracle in a cup'!

You can find a recipe using me on page 89.

Meet our Mulled Cider tea

A warming fruit tea packed with aromatic winter spices, including cinnamon, cloves and ginger, steeped with apple chunks, creating our mellow and comforting winter tea.

You can find a recipe using me on page 100.
We love this tea at Christmas; it's one of our limited edition winter blends so get it while it lasts!

Meet our Strawberry Lemonade tea

With real strawberry chunks, zesty lemon peel and a whole bunch of flavour, it's no wonder this blend is our bestselling fruit tea EVER. You never have to drink a fruit tea that tastes of nothing ever again because this zingy tea is sure to make everyone happy.

You can find recipes using me on pages 30, 101 and 103.
We love this tea cold brewed with fresh fruit – it's always on our drinks menus in our stores and on the road at festivals.

Meet our Blueberry & Peach tea

A fruity blend of peach and blueberries, this tea tastes like Ribena but with none of the added sugar and bursting with flavour.

We love this hot and cold brewed too. Why not use this blend to make a Bellini to perk up your day (recipe on page 105)?

Meet our Piña Colada tea

Inspired by the famous Piña Colada cocktail, this pretty blend will transport you to your dream holiday in the tropics with its creamy and refreshing coconut and pineapple flavour.

We love using this blend to make our version of a Piña Colada cocktail or mocktail (recipe on page 107).

Meet our Pure Grade Matcha tea

Matcha is traditional Japanese green tea, ground into a powder, which has been consumed for centuries for its green goodness. We use the highest quality traditional ground Japanese matcha powder which has been shaded two weeks prior to harvest. This is a classic ceremonial grade matcha, which is perfect for anything from traditional tea ceremonies to iced matcha lattes.

Matcha is a punchy ingredient to use in food recipes of all types: you can find recipes using me on pages 132-148. We love making matcha for ourselves and for our customers every day and recommend it hot as a frothy latte and iced as a thirst-quenching refreshment.

Meet our Lemon Matcha tea

This matcha blend was co-founder Krisi's first citrus matcha development, as she loved the benefits of matcha but wasn't a fan of the earthy taste. At the forefront of tea innovation, we have the largest selection of flavoured matcha in the UK. This matcha is one of our favourites to make an iced matcha lemonade with (recipe page 132), or to turn into a warming matcha latte with a splash of vanilla syrup – it tastes like a slice of lemon drizzle cake.

You can find recipes using me on pages 133 and 147.

Meet our Banana Bread Chai tea

This is our spiced chai perfection, hug in a mug blend with the perfect combination of banana, cinnamon, vanilla and cardamom.

We love this naturally caffeine-free tea hot with a splash of oat milk.
Use this tea to make the most sensational Banana Bread Chai Loaf (recipe on page 116). Can't you just smell it cooling straight from the oven?

Meet our Let's Be Having Brew! tea

All of our stores have their own loose leaf tea blend and Let's Be Having Brew is our Norwich store's blend. A rooibos tea base blended with Sri Lankan black tea and fenugreek with a smattering of sea buckthorn berries to give it a fruity boost. It's hearty, fruity and full of depth, just like Norwich.

You can find a recipe using me on page 128.

Meet our Apple Strudel tea

Another one of our award-winning blends, Apple Strudel tea, inspired by the classic *apfelstrudel* dessert, combines aromatic apple and cinnamon with a warming, spiced rooibos tea base. With real apple pieces, it's no surprise this naturally caffeine-free tea is popular with kids.

You can find a recipe using me on page 125.
We love this as a hot cuppa, with or without milk.

Meet our Birthday Cake tea

This naturally sweet, creamy rooibos blend is a birthday cake in a cup, sure to have you singing happy birthday to that special person.

You can find a recipe using me on page 127.
With tiny sprinkles dotted throughout, we love giving this tea as a gift, it's such a special treat for birthday celebrations big or small.

Meet our Gingerbread Chai tea

Our award-winning rooibos chai blend, created as homage to the Norwegian city of Bergen (they build a spectacular gingerbread city every Christmas), is the most delicious tea for Christmas as well as all year round. It's one of our bestsellers and an accessible gateway into the rest of our Tea Wall.

You can find recipes using me on pages 118 and 121.

THE BASICS

Cooking, baking and experimenting with tea

Getting started
20

———

HOW TO

Loose Leaf Tea
22

Tea Concentrate
25

Green Tea
26

Cold Brew
28

Iced Tea
29

Tea Lattes
32

Matcha Lattes
36

Wellness Teas
38

GETTING STARTED

How to use our tea to make delicious hot and cold drinks at home

We have tried and tested the best tools to make your loose leaf tea brewing journey a success, and we only recommend the ones we love and use ourselves:

The **Brewdini Gravity Steeper** was designed with best taste and no waste in mind. It is the perfect tool for fuss-free, drip-free and mess-free brewing! Using the Brewdini is a great way to add more depth to every brew, giving your tea leaves enough room to open up and really extract the full flavour. Simply pop it on a mug to filter through!

Our **Cold Brew Bottle** uses any cold liquid to infuse your tea slowly to extract more goodness, and produces a deliciously mild but flavourful drink. Just add 6 teaspoons of tea, fill it up with water, lemonade or your liquid of choice and leave it to infuse in the fridge for a minimum of 4 hours.

Our traditional **Bamboo Matcha Whisk** is the ultimate matcha making tool to make the perfect matcha green tea using a traditional technique.

Our **Matcha Milk Frother** helps to take your made-at-home lattes to the next level. This handheld frother tool whisks matcha to perfection, and can also be used to make super frothy milk for use in all your lattes.

Our **Loose Leaf Tea Infuser** is an essential tool for every tea cupboard! This universal tea infuser fits into most mugs, cups and pots. It is easy to use and mess-free, allowing you to brew without tea leaves coming into your cup. We prefer this infuser basket to a tea ball strainer as it gives more room for the tea leaves to brew.

Tip

There are so many different types of tea and they all have different optimal brewing temperatures. For example, green teas brew best with water at 80°C. Any hotter and they can taste burnt. To achieve this, just put a little bit of cold water onto the green tea leaves before adding boiling water.

HOW TO

Loose Leaf Tea

Making the perfect cup of loose leaf tea doesn't need
to be messy or complicated. With just a few tweaks and a bit
of love and attention we promise the resulting flavours you get
out of loose leaf tea are 100% worth it.

What you need

- Loose leaf tea of your choice (1 heaped teaspoon per person)
- You don't need fancy equipment to make a perfect cup of tea;
  most people have a mug and a spoon in their kitchens. It might
  be the infuser that seems a bit alien – we have our handy instructions
  for that.

How to brew loose leaf tea in a teapot

⇒ TA DA! ⇐

Add tea to infuser
Pop into teapot and add
correct water temperature

Pour into glass
when brewed

What to do

1. Place your loose leaf tea into an infuser or teapot. Be mindful of getting an even mixture of ingredients in your spoon. Some of the ingredients may settle in the bottom of your tin/pouch and some will float to the top over time, so give the packet a little shake first.

2. Check the desired brewing time and water temperature on the tea packet and fill your kettle with fresh water. Try to use only freshly boiled water each time and only fill the kettle with enough water for the tea you want to make (this saves a lot of energy). If the temperature guide says 80°C you can add a splash of cold water to the teapot before you fill it with freshly boiled water.

3. Set a timer from the moment the water hits the leaves. Leave to brew for the desired time, then strain. Once brewed, take out the infuser (if you've used one), throw away the leaves, give it a rinse and you'll have a beautiful, rich-tasting cup of tea!

4. You can then add any type of milk, if you desire. Some teas such as green teas are best enjoyed without milk, so be sure to check the brewing instructions that come with your tea.

Tip

Did you know you can place most used tea leaves into your garden compost and they will enrich the soil? Did you also know that you don't need to fully wash your strainer, teapot or infuser every time? Just a rinse will do on a day-to-day basis; we recommend a deeper clean once a week.

Easy tea brewing guide

There are different brewing times for different types of tea. But don't worry, we have a general rule of thumb:

 GREEN, WHITE AND OOLONG are delicate teas and need to be handled gently. They like 80°C water and brewing times of no longer than 3 minutes (otherwise they become bitter). If you don't have a fancy kettle that allows you to heat water to different temperatures, don't worry! Just add 1 part cold water to your mug and 4 parts boiling water. These teas are best enjoyed without milk.

BLACK TEAS need 100°C water and at least 4 minutes brewing time to let the full flavour develop, especially if you are adding milk. Let the leaves brew for the full time before adding the milk, otherwise the milk cools the water and you won't get a proper steep.

 All other **HERBAL TEAS**, **FRUIT TEAS** and **ROOIBOS TEAS** can be brewed with 100°C water and for as long as you want (for at least 4 minutes), but keep in mind that the longer you brew, the stronger the flavour. You can add milk to rooibos tea if you like.

Our **Brewdini Gravity Steepers** are the perfect way to make the ulTEAmate mess-free cuppa! We love them so much that we use them in all our stores to make all your favourite drinks. Not only do they give the tea leaves the space to brew that they deserve (giving you the best flavour) but they are super easy to use and clean.

MYTH BUSTER: Some people think that loose leaf tea is loads of hassle. But with the right infuser, it's not much more effort than a tea bag – for an even better flavour!

Tea Concentrate

The tea concentrate is used in many of our recipes. It's a great ingredient to have in your drinks arsenal: from iced cold drinks to glorious foamy lattes, you'll need a tea concentrate. But how do you make a tea concentrate? Well, read below to find out!

What you need

- Loose leaf tea of your choice (1 teaspoon to every 50ml of water)
- Boiling water (however much the recipe asks for)

What to do

1. Put your chosen tea into a Brewdini or tea strainer.

2. Add your boiling water (you may need to adjust the temperature depending on which type of tea you are using).

3. Allow the tea to steep for the brewing time outlined on the tea packet. Your tea concentrate will stay fresh for up to 3 days, so you can also store it for later.

Pick your recipe

If you want a **HOT LATTE**,
decant the tea into a mug and top up with hot foamy milk.

If you want an **ICED TEA LATTE**,
decant the tea into a glass and top up with ice and cold milk.

If you want to make an **ICED TEA WITH LEMONADE**,
decant the tea into a glass and top up with ice and lemonade.

HOW TO
Green Tea

Green tea has a bit of a bad rap. You might have heard about it. Maybe you've heard whispers that it's bitter? Goodness, no! We believe it's being done a massive disservice and all because a lot of people are still in the dark about the best way to make it. Green tea can seem super confusing, but it's our job to demystify it!

The secret to making the perfect green tea is all down to temperature and timing. Green tea is more delicate than black tea, so it needs a bit of gentle handling.

THE BEST GREEN TEAS
FOR BEGINNERS

Your ideal cup of green tea should have a green and fresh taste, as opposed to a bitter one: flavours can range from subtle to strong, grassy to vegetal and each variety of green tea has its own distinct flavour. Bird & Blend's green tea range is a great starting point for trying the different varieties; our fun flavours mean that we have something for everyone.

Three tips
for making green tea taste nice

Be very careful about temperature: too hot and you'll burn your leaves and that's what gives it the bitter taste. The perfect brewing temperature for green tea is around 80°C. We don't all have fancy kettles with different temperature settings, so this can be done in a couple of ways. The simplest is to put a splash of cold water into a mug before you top it up with freshly boiled water. Alternatively, you can switch the kettle off just before it starts boiling – as the noise of the kettle starts to increase.

The next thing a beginner needs to know about green tea is that **timing counts**! Brew too long and you'll have a bitter flavour that no one enjoys. Ideally, green tea should be brewed for no more than 3 minutes. Once you've removed the tea leaves, you're good to go!

Green tea is always best enjoyed **without milk**.

Tip

There are a few easy ways to choose the green tea blend for you: Japanese green tea would typically be steamed, which gives you an almost oceanic, fresh taste. Chinese green tea tends to be wok-fried, or oven-baked, giving it a nuttier flavour.

HOW TO
Cold Brew

We love iced tea, come rain or shine.
Our cold brewing teas are wonderfully
refreshing, low in sugar and delicious!
They're also super simple to make in
our cold brew bottle. Here's how:

How to cold brew tea

1 Scoop 5–6 teaspoons
into a bottle

2 Add 750ml
cold water

3 Leave 4–6 hrs
or overnight

4 Pour over
ice and enjoy!

Classic Iced Tea

Iced tea is the ultimate refresher. This timeless drink has a storied history, dating back to its accidental discovery at the 1904 St Louis World's Fair. Richard Blechynden realised that the summer heat meant that no one wanted hot tea, so he ran the tea through iced lead pipes and it was a hit! Nowadays, iced tea is synonymous with summer, and we can't help but love it!

SERVES 1 | **PREP** 5 mins

2–4 heaped tsp loose leaf tea (we recommend any of the teas in our **COLD BREW TEA** collection)
100ml boiling water
Ice cubes
Water or lemonade
Sweeteners or garnish, such as syrup, lemon slices or mint (optional)

1. Add your chosen tea to a Brewdini or tea strainer.

2. Top up with the boiling water, following the tea's brewing instructions on temperature.

3. Allow to steep for 3–4 minutes, following the tea's brewing instructions, then strain.

4. Pour over ice and top up with water or lemonade.

5. Add sweeteners or garnish if desired.

6. Enjoy!

Strawberry Lemonade Iced Tea

Oh, that perfect summer drink! Refreshing, thirst-quenching and super fruity, our Strawberry Lemonade Iced Tea is guaranteed to bring sunshine to your day. If you're feeling cheeky, add a little vodka and you have an incredible summer cocktail.

SERVES 1-2 | **PREP** 5 mins

4 heaped tsp
STRAWBERRY LEMONADE blend
300ml boiling water
3 tsp syrup or sweetener of your choice
1 cup of ice
4 strawberries, halved
1 lemon, quartered
200ml lemonade or sparkling water

1. Brew the tea in a Brewdini or tea strainer with the boiling water for at least 4 minutes.

2. Strain the tea and place in the fridge to cool. Alternatively, you can put the steeping tea in the fridge overnight and strain the following day (for an extra strong taste).

3. When it's cooled down you can stir in your chosen sweetener.

4. When ready to serve, half-fill one or two glasses with ice and pop in a few strawberries and two lemon wedges (don't forget to squeeze the juice).

5. Add the Strawberry Lemonade tea to the glasses and top up with lemonade or sparkling water.

6. Stir well, and enjoy!

Iced Chai

We serve up our iced chai at festivals and events throughout the summer, as well as year-round in our stores. Don't worry if you can't get to us though – with this easy recipe you can make your own iced chai at home.

SERVES 1-2 | **PREP** 5 mins

4 heaped tsp chai (we use our **TOFFEE CHAI** blend)
300ml boiling water
1 tbsp sweetener of your choice (optional)
1 cup of ice
100ml milk of your choice (we use whole dairy or oat milk)
1 tsp ground cinnamon

1. Brew the chai in a Brewdini or tea strainer with the boiling water for at least 4 minutes. We sweeten it at this point, which you can do too if desired.

2. Strain the chai and place in the fridge to cool. Alternatively, you can put the steeping tea in the fridge overnight and strain the following day (for an extra strong taste).

3. When ready to serve, fill one or two glasses with ice, pour in the chai and top up with milk.

4. Sprinkle with the cinnamon and enjoy!

MYTH BUSTER: iced tea isn't just for people who don't like hot tea, and it's not just made with black tea or heaps of sugar. Herbal and fruit iced teas are even more refreshing - and virtually sugar-free!

Moondrop Dreams Iced Latte

It's super easy to turn your favourite tea into a latte – iced or hot. Here's a couple of our favourite recipes to show you how, starting with our Moondrop Dreams Iced Latte! This caffeine-free wonder is sure to have you floating on a cloud in no time.

SERVES 1 | **PREP** 5 mins

2 heaped tsp **MOONDROP DREAMS** blend
150ml boiling water
1 cup of ice
1 tsp sweetener of your choice
150ml milk of your choice
A pinch of lavender (optional)

1. First, brew the tea with the boiling water in a Brewdini or tea strainer for 4 minutes.

2. In the meantime, get the ice ready by popping it into a cocktail shaker. Once your tea has brewed, add the tea to the shaker along with your chosen sweetener.

3. Shake, shake, shake! Then pour the contents into a glass and top up with cold milk. Top with a pinch of lavender if desired. Sit back, relax and enjoy!

Earl Grey Creme Latte

Creamy and succulent, your favourite brew transformed into an indulgent latte. Learn how to make one of our favourite in-store drinks, the Earl Grey Creme Latte. This will blow your mind with every sip. It really is as delicious as it sounds.

SERVES 1 | **PREP** 5 mins

2 heaped tsp **EARL GREY CREME** blend
150ml boiling water
150ml milk of your choice
1 tsp sweetener of your choice

1. First, brew the tea with the boiling water in a Brewdini or tea strainer for 4 minutes.

2. In the meantime, heat your milk – be careful not to make it piping hot!

3. Whisk the milk until frothy with fine bubbles for the perfect latte texture. You can use an electric whisk to get this extra frothy!

4. Pour the tea into a cup and add sweetener if desired. Now pour in your frothed milk, making sure you get a big dollop of foam on top. Enjoy!

The Best Chai Latte

Add a little spice to your day with this delicious recipe. You can apply this method to any chai you like, to make the perfect thick, foamy latte. Chai is traditionally brewed in milk, but this is a quick and easy way to make it at home.

SERVES 1-2   **PREP** 5 mins

3 heaped tsp chai (we use our **GINGERBREAD CHAI** blend)
300ml boiling water
150ml milk of your choice
1 tbsp honey or syrup (we love cinnamon or vanilla, optional)
Ground cinnamon

1. Brew the tea in a Brewdini or tea strainer with the boiling water for 4 minutes.

2. In the meantime, heat the milk in a pan on the hob or in the microwave until it's nice and hot.

3. Using a handheld milk frother, foam the milk until it's nice and thick.

4. Add the tea to your favourite mug and add honey or syrup if you like.

5. Pour the foamy milk on to your tea, adding a nice big dollop of frothy milk on the top.

6. Sprinkle with some cinnamon and enjoy!

Chocolate Indulgent Latte

The chocolate digestive, arguably the top of the biscuit pyramid. Learn how to make this indulgently decadent mega latte from the comfort of your own home. Take it to the next level and create your own ultimate Chocolate Digestives latte – a velvety smooth, caramel and chocolate delight.

SERVES 1 | **PREP** 5 mins

2 heaped tsp chocolate-flavoured loose leaf black tea (we use our **CHOCOLATE DIGESTIVES** blend)
150ml boiling water
150ml milk of your choice (we use oat milk)
1 tsp sweetener of your choice (we use honey)

SUPERSIZE YOUR LATTE WITH THESE OPTIONAL TOPPINGS
Whipped cream
Cocoa powder
Chocolate digestive biscuits, crumbled

1. Brew the tea in a Brewdini or tea strainer with the boiling water for 4 minutes.

2. Pour the tea into a large mug, leaving enough room for the milk and toppings.

3. Gently heat the milk on the hob and use a milk frother or a latte whisk to froth it.

4. Now you can add a teaspoonful of honey (or your chosen sweetener) to your tea and give it a stir. Then pour the milk over the tea, making sure you get a lovely big dollop of foam on top.

5. If you like you can finish your latte with whipped cream, cocoa powder and a crumble of chocolate digestive biscuits. Enjoy!

Iced Vanilla Matcha Latte

Learn how to make one of the easiest, yet most delicious matcha drinks we've tried. Our iced vanilla matcha latte is so tasty, we'll be drinking it all summer long!

SERVES 1 | **PREP** 5 mins

½ tsp **PURE GRADE MATCHA**
150ml 80°C water
1 cup of ice
Vanilla extract
150ml almond milk (or milk of your choice)

1. Add the matcha to a mug or cup. Add a little of the 80°C water and whisk well to get rid of any lumps. If you don't have a fancy kettle that allows you to heat water to 80°C, just add a splash of cold water before you add the just-boiled water. The best (and the traditional way) of doing this is with a bamboo matcha whisk but you can use a battery-powered whisk instead.

2. When the matcha is smooth and there are no lumps, pour the matcha shot over a glass of ice.

3. Add a few drops of vanilla extract, then fill up your glass with milk and stir. Enjoy!

MYTH BUSTER: Some people think that matcha tastes grassy and not very nice. But if it's made right, the flavour is lovely! If it tastes bitter, this is just because it has been burnt by too-hot water.

The Perfect Matcha Latte

Calling all matcha fans, we have a scrumptious blend for you! Get your hands on a tin of our Ice Cream Matcha – the perfect treat that'll satisfy any sweet tooth. I scream, you scream, we all scream for an Ice Cream Matcha Latte...

SERVES 1　　　　　　**PREP** 5 mins

1 tsp matcha (we use our **ICE CREAM MATCHA** blend)
100ml 80°C water
Vanilla extract (optional)
1 tsp honey (optional)
100ml milk of your choice (we use oat milk)
Coloured sprinkles
Cone and flake (optional)

1. Add the matcha to a mug or cup. Add a little of the 80°C water and whisk well to get rid of any lumps. If you don't have a fancy kettle that allows you to heat water to 80°C, just add a splash of cold water before you add the just-boiled water. The best (and the traditional way) of doing this is with a bamboo matcha whisk but you can use a battery-powered whisk instead.

2. When smooth, add water until half-full. Stir in a few drops of vanilla extract and honey, if using.

3. Next, gently heat and froth the milk in a saucepan on the hob (if you are using a handheld milk frother, you can add the milk directly to the tea and then froth for a creamier taste).

4. Add the milk to the tea, stirring as you go and ensuring you get a nice big dollop of frothy milk on top. Add some coloured sprinkles for a fun effect!

5. Top with an ice cream cone and a flake, if that's what you fancy.

The Digester

This recipe is made using our amazing digestive blend, developed especially with those suffering from IBS, bloating and sluggish metabolisms in mind. With loads of natural ingredients that help with gut health, we recommend drinking this after a large evening meal.

SERVES 1 | **PREP** 5 mins

1 tea bag or 1 heaped tsp
   loose leaf **THE DIGESTER**
   blend
300ml boiling water
1 slice of fresh ginger
1 slice of orange
1 tsp honey

1. Brew the tea in a Brewdini or tea strainer with the boiling water for 3–4 minutes. If using a tea bag just add this to your favourite cup or mug along with the boiling water.

2. Add the ginger and orange to your mug, along with the honey.

3. Strain the tea into the mug, and give it a stir.

4. Enjoy!

Immunity Warrior

Our Cold Weather Warrior tea contains echinacea and eucalyptus, great for tackling a cold and for building immunity during the colder seasons. It also has aniseed, chilli and peppermint to really clear out those sinuses.

SERVES 1 | **PREP** 5 mins

1 tea bag or 1 heaped tsp loose leaf **COLD WEATHER WARRIOR** blend
300ml boiling water
1 tsp honey
1 slice of lemon
1 handful of fresh mint leaves

1. Brew the tea in a Brewdini or tea strainer with the boiling water for 3–4 minutes. If using a tea bag just add this to your favourite cup or mug along with the boiling water.

2. Slice your lemon and prep your mint, adding them to your mug, along with the honey.

3. Strain the tea into the mug, and give it a stir.

4. Enjoy!

Sore Throat Soother

Lemon and honey are both great for soothing itchy and sore throats and ginger is a staple for when you need to beat a cold or cough. When combined in a warming mug of tea this recipe is sure to bring your sore throat some relief.

SERVES 1 | **PREP** 5 mins

1 tea bag or 1 heaped
tsp loose leaf **LEMON &
GINGER** tea
300ml boiling water
1 tsp honey
1/2 lemon
2 slices of fresh ginger

1. Brew the tea in a Brewdini or tea strainer with the boiling water for 3–4 minutes. If using a tea bag just add this to your favourite cup or mug along with the boiling water.

2. Add the honey, lemon and ginger to your mug.

3. Strain the tea into the mug, and give it a stir.

4. Enjoy!

Ingwer Tea

This is a ginger tea with a twist, though this recipe is great with any herbal blend as its base. You can choose from the optional add-ons to build the perfect herbal tea for you. We really love using orange, ginger and mint to create a delicious soothing brew for any weather.

SERVES 1 | **PREP** 5 mins

1 tea bag or 1 heaped tsp loose leaf **LEMON & GINGER, COLD WEATHER WARRIOR** or **DECKCHAIR DREAMING**
300ml boiling water

OPTIONAL ADDITIONS:
1 slice of fresh ginger
1 slice of lemon
1 slice of orange
1 small handful of fresh mint leaves
1 tsp honey

1. Brew the tea in a Brewdini or tea strainer with the boiling water for 3–4 minutes. If using a tea bag just add this to your favourite cup or mug along with the boiling water.

2. Add your chosen additions to your mug.

3. Strain the tea into the mug, and give it a stir.

4. Enjoy!

BLACK

If you'd like to add an incredible depth of flavour and richness to your cooking then these recipes using black tea as an ingredient are definitely for you. Using some of our most popular and award-winning black teas, including Earl Grey Creme, Chocolate Digestives and Smoky Russian, these recipes are ideal for special occasions or simply for sharing with friends.

Although black tea contains caffeine, when it is used as an ingredient in a bake, for example, the caffeine level changes, with much less caffeine in the end product. So even if you don't drink black tea, cooking and baking with black tea won't yield caffeine-fuelled food, rather a flavourful tea-infused treat you can enjoy any time of the day. With all of these recipes, you can substitute any similar flavoured, good quality black tea. We've included bakes, celebration cocktails or mocktails, savoury bites and seasonal specials.

THE BEST BOOZY
BREAKFAST COCKTAIL

Serves 1

This boozy breakfast cocktail made with our Smoky Russian tea will leave you utterly speechless, it's that good. A delightfully smoky and surprising way to start your holiday or begin a festive day.

PREP 5 mins + cooling | **NO COOK**

3 heaped tsp black tea (we use our **SMOKY RUSSIAN** blend)
100ml boiling water
1 tbsp fine-cut orange marmalade
60ml gin
Juice of ½ orange, plus twist of rind to garnish
1 tsp agave syrup
A handful of ice

Step 1
Brew the tea in a Brewdini or tea strainer with the boiling water for 2–4 minutes, then strain into a bowl with the marmalade and stir until it dissolves. Leave to cool. This will make a tea marmalade concentrate.

Step 2
Add the gin, orange juice, agave syrup and 30ml of the tea concentrate to a cocktail shaker, along with the ice. Shake until the shaker feels cold and then strain into a martini glass. Finish with a twist of orange rind.

EARL GREY YOGHURT LOAF

This scrumptiously moist loaf made with Earl Grey tea is the perfect sharing treat for you and your guests. Serve this beautiful bake warm or cold and pair it with our Choccy Biccy Milk Tea (see page 52) – it's absolutely lush!

PREP 15 mins | **COOK** 1 hour

240g plain flour
A pinch of salt
½ tsp baking powder
½ tsp bicarbonate of soda
2 large eggs
225g caster sugar
225g natural yoghurt
2 tsp vanilla extract
9 tsp Earl Grey tea (we use our **EARL GREY CREME** blend)
200ml vegetable oil, plus extra for greasing
1 tbsp demerara sugar
Dried cornflower petals, to garnish

Step 1
Preheat the oven to 190°C/170°C fan. Grease a 900g loaf tin with vegetable oil and line with baking paper, leaving an overhang to help you remove the loaf later. Whisk the flour, salt, baking powder and bicarbonate of soda in a bowl to combine. Set aside.

Step 2
In a separate bowl, whisk the eggs and caster sugar for about a minute until pale and foamy.

Step 3
Whisk the yoghurt and vanilla extract into the eggs and sugar mixture. Stir in the tea leaves – you may want to give them a scrunch before adding them in, to break down any large leaves.

Step 4
Gradually stream in the vegetable oil, whisking constantly until incorporated. Add the dry ingredients and whisk the mixture until combined and lightly speckled with tea leaves.

Step 5

Pour the mixture into the prepared loaf tin and lightly tap the tin on the worktop, to get rid of any big air bubbles. Sprinkle the top of the loaf with the demerara sugar for a nice crunch.

Step 6

Pop the loaf into the oven and bake for 1 hour, or until a skewer inserted into the centre comes out clean. You may have to cover it with foil three-quarters of the way through if it's turning brown quickly. Leave to cool completely in the tin.

Step 7

Use the baking paper to remove the loaf from the tin. Garnish with a few cornflower petals, if using.

CHOCCY BICCY MILK TEA

The decadent alternative way to enjoy a chocolate digestive biscuit, made with our award-winning Chocolate Digestives tea. This is definitely one of our best-loved black tea blends, with cocoa shells and nibs, fenugreek and liquorice root.

PREP 5 mins | **NO COOK**

150ml black tea concentrate (see page 25 – we use our **CHOCOLATE DIGESTIVES** blend)
1 tsp cocoa powder, plus extra (optional) for dusting
25ml vanilla syrup
1 cup of ice
Milk of your choice, to top up

OPTIONAL TOPPINGS
½ chocolate biscuit, crumbled
Whipped cream
Chocolate syrup and crushed chocolate chip cookies (approx. ½ biscuit per glass)

Step 1
Add the tea concentrate, cocoa powder and vanilla syrup to a cocktail shaker, along with the ice, and shake to combine the ingredients. Strain into a glass and top up with milk.

Step 2
Half a chocolate biscuit crumbled on top works well as a topping. You can add whipped cream if you wish. A dusting of cocoa powder also looks good.

Step 3
If you want to take things up a notch, before filling the glass, paint the rim with chocolate syrup and dip and roll the edge into a plate of finely crushed chocolate chip cookie crumbs.

G & TEA

A lively and modern twist on the quintessential gin cocktail and you can use any Earl Grey you prefer. You can also substitute for one of our herbal teas such as Champagne Supernova, Deep Breaths or Bedknobs & Broomsticks. Refreshing, classic, tasty. Enough said.

PREP 12–48 hours
(for infusing)

NO COOK

6–7 heaped tsp tea
    blend of your choice,
    depending on desired
    strength
70cl bottle of gin
Ice
150ml lemonade
Slice of lemon or lime
Cold brew bottle

Step 1
Add the tea to a cold brew bottle (see page 20).

Step 2
Add the gin. Set aside for 12–48 hours at room temperature, depending on your desired depth of flavour.

Step 3
Fill a cup with ice. Add 25ml of the tea-infused gin. Top up with the lemonade. Add a slice of lemon or lime and enjoy!

Tip

Not all teas need boiling water!

SMOKY TEA STEAK

Serves 2

Rethink the classic dish with this smoky tea-infused steak recipe. This is a unique and flavourful recipe, perfect for a special occasion or a weekend barbecue. Serve with chips and a peppery rocket salad.

PREP 5 mins + marination | **COOK** 6 mins + resting

2 tbsp black tea (we use our **SMOKY RUSSIAN** blend)
½ tbsp black peppercorns, finely ground
2 tsp onion granules
2 tsp garlic granules
1½ tsp sea salt
2 x 250g steaks (we use sirloin)
1 tsp vegetable oil
Chips and a rocket salad, to serve (optional)

Step 1
Grind the tea, peppercorns, onion and garlic granules and salt in a pestle and mortar or spice grinder to make your spice mix.

Step 2
Rub the spice mix onto the steaks and leave to marinate in the fridge overnight.

Step 3
To cook, heat the oil in a frying pan over a high heat and fry the steaks for 2–3 minutes on each side for medium rare. Leave to rest for 2 minutes, then slice. Serve with your choice of sides.

THE ULTIMATE PUMPKIN SPICED LATTE

Our bestselling autumnal drink, made with our award-winning spiced-to-perfection Spiced Pumpkin Pie tea. This is a fan favourite and cosy staple, especially during the spooky season, when our customers cannot get enough!

PREP 5 mins | **NO COOK**

100ml black tea or chai concentrate (see page 25 – we use our **SPICED PUMPKIN PIE** blend)
25ml honey
25ml cinnamon syrup
150ml dairy or oat milk
Whipped cream
Sprinkles (optional)

TO SERVE (OPTIONAL)
Grated nutmeg
1 cinnamon stick
1 star anise

Step 1
Add the tea concentrate, honey, syrup and milk to a large mug. Froth, froth, froth using a handheld milk frother.

Step 2
Top with whipped cream and sprinkles, if using.

Step 3
If you like, you can grate over some fresh nutmeg and garnish with a cinnamon stick and a star anise.

AUTUMN SPICED CARAMEL BUNDT CAKE

This Bundt cake is made with our most popular autumn tea, Spiced Pumpkin Pie. It's soft, cosy and spectacular, with a decadent caramel glaze. You can substitute any black tea or chai. Absolutely delicious! This recipe was inspired by Brewbird Maddy.

PREP 15 mins (+ 30 mins steeping + 1 hour chilling for infused butter)	**COOK** 35–45 mins (+ 5 mins for infused butter)

250g unsalted butter, plus extra for greasing
4 tbsp black tea or chai (we use our **SPICED PUMPKIN PIE** blend)
250g caster sugar
100g light brown sugar
1 tsp baking powder
¼ tsp bicarbonate of soda
350g plain flour
1 tsp salt
2 tsp ground cinnamon
1 tsp ground nutmeg
1 tsp ground cardamom
½ tsp ground black pepper
3 large eggs
200g full-fat natural yoghurt
1 tsp vanilla extract

FOR THE CARAMEL DRIZZLE
200g dark brown sugar
½ x 397g tin condensed milk
55g unsalted butter
1 tsp vanilla extract
75ml double cream

Step 1

You can make the infused tea butter in advance. In a saucepan, add the butter and chai tea leaves and heat gently, stirring until the butter is melted. Take off the heat and leave to cool for 30 minutes or so – the longer you leave it to infuse, the stronger the chai flavour.

Step 2

The tea butter mix will have started to solidify on cooling, so gently reheat until it is liquid again. Strain the butter into a mixing bowl. Press the tea leaves with the back of a spoon to extract as much butter as you can and scrape any excess from the bottom of the sieve. Discard the tea leaves. You can now leave the butter to re-solidify in the bowl, placing it in the fridge for 30 minutes or so if you want to speed up the process. Remember, it's always good to work with room temperature butter to make cakes, so if it's in the fridge, make sure you take it out at least 1 hour before baking.

Step 3

Preheat the oven to 195°C/175°C fan and thoroughly grease a 23cm Bundt tin, 1.5 litres in volume. This step is really important to ensure the sponge doesn't stick – make sure you get into all the crevices of the tin.

Step 4

In a mixing bowl with an electric whisk or using a freestanding mixer, beat together 175g of the tea-infused butter and both sugars until light and fluffy; about 5 minutes. Meanwhile, sift the baking powder, bicarbonate of soda, flour, salt and spices into a bowl.

Step 5

Beat in the eggs, one at a time, to the butter and sugar, then beat for a minute and add a spoonful of the sifted dry ingredients if it begins to curdle slightly. Scrape down the sides of the bowl. Add the yoghurt and vanilla extract, briefly whisking to combine.

Step 6

Stir in the remaining flour and spices, scraping the sides and bottom of the bowl, and beat briefly to incorporate any residue.

Step 7

Scoop the batter into the prepared tin, even out the top using a small spatula and bake for 35–45 minutes until golden brown. It's worth checking the cake after 35 minutes. If it is browning but not cooked, carefully cover it with a layer of foil to stop the top from burning.

Step 8

Remove the cake from the oven and leave to cool in the tin for 15 minutes before turning it out onto a rack to cool completely.

Step 9

To make the caramel, add the brown sugar and condensed milk to a large saucepan over a medium-low heat. Stir constantly until the sugar dissolves, then remove from the heat. This will take at least 5 minutes.

Step 10

Add the butter and vanilla extract to the sugar mixture and stir well until the butter melts.

Step 11

Slowly stir in the double cream and continue stirring until everything is fully incorporated and has created a glossy caramel. Place the cake on a wire rack with a plate underneath. Drizzle the caramel over the sponge. Allow to set slightly for 5 minutes, then carefully transfer to a plate to serve. Serve any leftover caramel on the side.

GREEN

Green tea has seen a huge rise in popularity due to its perceived health benefits and versatility, and the recipes in this chapter – made with our flavourful citrus, fruity and floral green tea blends – will unleash your creativity in the kitchen.

You'll notice that in these recipes, the method for brewing green tea is different to brewing black and other types of tea. This is quite important and, as tea mixologists, is something we are passionate about telling people about. There have been countless times when customers tell us they don't like the taste of green tea, saying that it's too bitter. When we tell them that green tea needs to be brewed using water at at 80°C, not boiling water as that burns the tea leaves, and offer them a sample, they are absolutely delighted and often go on to become green tea drinkers. You'll be amazed to discover these wonderful and harmonious dishes and drinks using green tea as a key ingredient.

BLACKCURRANT GREEN TEA SPRITZ

A refreshing, fruity, pick-me-up spritz with a difference, giving you that little bit extra. Made with green tea balanced with sweet blackcurrant, this is light and flavourful. You can use whichever of our green tea blends you prefer!

PREP 5 mins | **NO COOK**

100ml green tea concentrate (see page 25, you can use any green tea here)
25ml blackcurrant cordial (we use Ribena)
2 blackberries
A scoop of ice
Sparkling water or lemonade

Step 1
In a shaker, add the green tea concentrate, blackcurrant cordial, blackberries and ice. Shake, shake, shake.

Step 2
Pour into your chosen glass and top with sparkling water, or if you like it really sweet, some lemonade.

GREEN TEA MISO SOUP

This nourishing miso soup is made using our Chinese Treasures tea but you can substitute any other green tea, including our MojiTEA or Ankara Apple. Add tofu, mushrooms, green beans or whatever veg you fancy.

PREP 5 mins | **COOK** 15 mins

4 tsp green tea (we use our **CHINESE TREASURES** blend)
A splash of cold water
700ml boiling water
2 tbsp white miso paste
300g block silken tofu, cut into 2cm cubes

OPTIONAL GARNISHES
Drizzle of sesame oil
Sliced spring onions
Sprinkle of toasted sesame seeds
Sliced red chillies

Step 1
Brew the tea in a Brewdini or tea strainer with the cold water, immediately followed by the boiling water, for 3 minutes, then strain into a pan. Add the white miso and bring to the boil.

Step 2
Divide between four bowls and top with the silken tofu and garnishes of your choice.

GREEN TEA LATTE

Serves 1

This is a healthy, flavourful drink, perfect at any time of the day, especially if you're looking for a hot and refreshing pick-me-up! Any green tea will work here, but we like it with our Chinese Treasures blend. Just make sure you use 80°C water instead of boiling or you'll burn the tea.

PREP 5 mins | **NO COOK**

½ tbsp green tea (we use our **CHINESE TREASURES** blend)
A splash of cold water
250ml boiling water
100ml milk (we use semi-skimmed but you can use a plant-based alternative)
1½ tsp honey
A pinch of ground ginger, cinnamon and nutmeg

Step 1
Brew the green tea leaves in a Brewdini or tea strainer with the cold water, immediately followed by the boiling water, for 3 minutes.

Step 2
While your tea is brewing, heat your chosen milk in a saucepan on the hob, or in the microwave, then foam it up with a handheld milk frother.

Step 3
Strain the tea into a mug and add the milk, honey and spices. Give it a stir, and enjoy!

MOJITEA

Say hello to your new best-loved cocktail, the ultimate minty iced tea drink! Brought to you from our in-store drinks menu, this amazing iced tea recipe uses our green tea blend MojiTEA (Mojito-tea, ya get it?!) and the result is a beautiful chorus of refreshing, zingy lime and mint flavours.

PREP 5 mins | **NO COOK**

A handful of mint, torn
Juice of ¼ lime
3 lime slices
150ml green tea concentrate (see page 25 – we use our **MojiTEA** blend)
25ml white rum
Glass of ice

Step 1
Add the mint, lime juice, two of the lime slices, green tea concentrate, white rum (if using) and ice to a cocktail shaker. Shake it, baby!

Step 2
Pour into your chosen glass and garnish with the remaining slice of lime.

GREEN TEA GIMLET

Serves 2

A classy tea cocktail made using any green tea with refreshing citrus undertones paired perfectly with the vodka for a silky smooth liquid infusion. You can use any green tea you like. Pitcher ready, you'll be the envy of the party!

PREP 3 mins + infusing | **NO COOK**

Juice of 1 lime (use the peel to garnish)
30–60ml agave or sugar syrup
A handful of ice
Twist of lime peel, to garnish

FOR THE INFUSED VODKA
750ml good-quality vodka
6 tsp green tea (we use our **ANKARA APPLE** blend)

Step 1
To make the infused vodka, funnel the tea leaves into the bottle of vodka, place the cap on and shake well. Leave to steep for 10 hours, then strain.

Step 2
Put 120ml of the infused vodka, the lime juice, agave or sugar syrup and ice into a cocktail shaker. Shake until the cocktail shaker feels cold and then strain into a glass.

Step 3
Garnish with the twist of lime peel.

GREEN TEA POACHED PEARS

This naturally sweet pear dish is beautifully flavoured using our Chinese Treasures tea, a powerful blend of jasmine green, ginseng and subtle spices. You can use any green tea here. Go on, you know you want to make this!

PREP 5 mins | **COOK** 15–25 mins

2 tbsp green tea (we use our **CHINESE TREASURES** blend)
500ml water
1 tsp lemon juice
A few strips of lemon peel
1 cinnamon stick
A few cardamom pods
1 star anise
2 firm pears (Bosc or Conference are best), peeled, halved and cored
150g caster sugar

TO SERVE (OPTIONAL)
Natural yoghurt
Granola

Step 1
Put the tea leaves in a Bird & Blend tea infuser sac (or use a green tea bag) in a pan with the water and lemon juice and heat until steaming. Add the strips of lemon peel, cinnamon stick, cardamom pods and star anise.

Step 2
Add the pears to the pan so that they are covered by the liquid, and bring to a gentle simmer. Poach gently until cooked through (check with a sharp knife). This should take 15–25 minutes.

Step 3
Remove the pears and the tea bag from the liquid and add the sugar to the pan. Bring to the boil and reduce until the liquid becomes syrupy.

Step 4
Serve the pears warm or cold with yoghurt and granola, if using, and a drizzle of syrup. The pears and syrup will keep in the fridge for up to 2 days.

OOLONG

We love oolong tea with its subtle flavour notes that last and last – you can rebrew this tea up to seven times, so one serving can last you all day. Oolong tea sits between a green and a black tea, in terms of strength, brewing methods and processing methods. Drinking oolong tea can be good for your gut too. Oolong teas are partly oxidised (green teas do not oxidise and black teas are 'fully' oxidised), so they have enough caffeine to activate the gut, and are also packed full of polyphenols and antioxidants to fight off the bad stuff!

There are many different types of oolong, but they all share a smooth, creamy, earthy flavour, and can be transformed into a wide variety of delicious beverages, energy-boosting refreshers and gorgeous showstopping desserts. And, because they can be rebrewed, you can enjoy a delicious creamy cuppa before or after making one of these recipes!

PEPPERMINT AND CHOCOLATE CAKE

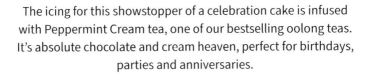

The icing for this showstopper of a celebration cake is infused with Peppermint Cream tea, one of our bestselling oolong teas. It's absolute chocolate and cream heaven, perfect for birthdays, parties and anniversaries.

PREP 35 mins + cooling | **COOK** 35 mins

200g natural yoghurt
Juice of ½ lemon
150ml olive oil
200ml brewed coffee, cooled slightly
2 large eggs
1 tsp vanilla bean paste
275g self-raising flour
50g cocoa powder
1 tsp bicarbonate of soda
150g caster sugar
150g soft dark brown sugar
A pinch of sea salt flakes

FOR THE ICING
4 tsp oolong tea (we use our **PEPPERMINT CREAM** blend)
100ml 80 °C water
500g icing sugar
250g unsalted butter, softened
Green gel food colouring (optional)
A handful of fresh mint leaves (optional)

Step 1

Preheat the oven to 180°C/160°C fan and line 2 x 20cm round cake tins with baking paper. Put the yoghurt and lemon juice in a mixing bowl, stir, then leave to sit for 3 minutes. Whisk in the oil, coffee, eggs and vanilla bean paste.

Step 2

In another bowl, combine the flour, cocoa powder, bicarbonate of soda, both sugars and salt, mixing with your fingers to break up any sugar clumps. Mix the wet ingredients into the dry until you have a smooth batter.

Step 3

Divide between the prepared tins and spread so they're level. Bake for 30–35 minutes until a skewer inserted into the centre comes out clean. Leave to cool in the tins for 10 minutes before removing from the tins and leaving to cool completely.

continues overleaf

Step 4

For the icing, brew the tea in the water for 3 minutes to make a strong concentrate. Using an electric whisk, whisk the icing sugar and butter together until pale and fluffy. Then beat in around half of the brewed tea until you have a soft icing that still holds its shape.

Step 5

If you like, you can paint stripes of green food colouring on the inside of a piping bag and then spoon in the icing. Place one sponge onto a plate and pipe blobs around the top of the sponge until it's covered. Put the other sponge on top and continue to pipe dots on top until covered. Finish with a few mint leaves.

HOT CHOCO-LATTE

Decadent and frothy, this hot latte made
with our Peppermint Cream tea and coconut milk
(or your preferred hot milk) will soothe you at any time of day. You've
got this! You can also use any other type of oolong tea.

PREP 5 mins   **COOK** 5 mins

2 tsp oolong tea (we use
   our **PEPPERMINT CREAM**
   blend)
100ml boiling water
1 tsp cocoa powder
Vanilla syrup
100ml coconut milk

Step 1
Brew the tea in a Brewdini or tea strainer with the
boiling water for 4 minutes, then strain into a mug.

Step 2
Add the cocoa powder, then a pump of vanilla
syrup.

Step 3
Heat the coconut milk in a saucepan on the
hob, or in the microwave, then foam it up with
a handheld milk frother.

Step 4
Pour the frothy milk over the tea concentrate
mixture, then enjoy!

TEA LOAF

Here's a beautifully aromatic, tea-infused version
of the classic fruit loaf, perfect for breakfast with a hot cuppa
or for a mid afternoon tea break with a refreshing iced tea on the side.
Either way, you'll want a thick slice! This can also be made with any
black or oolong tea blend.

PREP 15 mins + cooling | **COOK** 1½ hours

3 tbsp oolong or black
tea (we use our **MILK
OOLONG CHAI** blend)
300ml boiling water
340g mixed dried fruit (we
like to use a mixture of
sultanas, cranberries and
mixed peel)
Zest and juice of 1 lemon
2 medium eggs
200g light soft brown sugar
50g unsalted butter,
melted, plus extra for
greasing and to serve
250g self-raising flour

Step 1
Preheat the oven to 180°C/160°C fan and grease
and line a 900g loaf tin with baking paper.

Step 2
Brew the tea in a Brewdini or tea strainer with the
boiling water for 3 minutes. Put the dried fruit,
lemon zest and juice into a saucepan and strain the
tea into the pan. Bring to the boil, then take off the
heat, tip into a large mixing bowl and leave to cool
completely.

Step 3
Once cool, mix in the eggs, sugar and butter and
then fold in the flour.

Step 4
Tip into the prepared tin and cook for 1½ hours.
Leave to cool in the tin for 30 minutes and then tip
out onto a wire rack and leave to cool completely.
Slice and serve with butter.

OMBRE
ICE LOLLIES

These milk chai ice lollies will positively invigorate your day. Why not try them for a refreshing, naturally sweet mid-afternoon or evening treat? These can be made with any oolong or chai, including our Toffee Chai or Carrot Cake tea.

PREP 10 mins + freezing | **COOK** 5 mins

270ml coconut milk, whisked to combine if separated
2 tbsp maple syrup
1 tbsp vanilla bean paste
300ml oat or dairy milk
3 tbsp oolong tea or chai (we use our **MILK OOLONG CHAI** blend)

Step 1
Whisk the coconut milk with 1 tablespoon of the maple syrup and the vanilla bean paste. Pour it into 9 lolly moulds, filling each one halfway. Then leave in the freezer for at least 2 hours to set.

Step 2
Add the milk, tea and remaining tablespoon of maple syrup to a saucepan and heat until just about simmering. Turn off the heat and leave the tea to infuse for at least 30 minutes. Strain the tea when it's reached your desired intensity, pushing the tea leaves down to get all the flavour out of them.

Step 3
Take the lolly moulds out of the freezer and pour the tea mixture on top of the frozen coconut milk, place the lolly sticks in and leave in the freezer overnight.

Step 4
To release the lollies, dip the moulds very briefly in hot water and they will easily slide out.

OOLONG WHITE RUSSIAN

Serves
1

A warming wintry chai cocktail to make your day pop!
Made with our popular Milk Oolong Chai tea with ginger,
cinnamon, cocoa shells and chilli, this flavour combination will
capture your imagination and quell your craving.

PREP 5 mins + cooling | **NO COOK**

2 tsp oolong tea or chai
(we use our **MILK
OOLONG CHAI** blend)
100ml boiling water
1 tsp hot chocolate
powder
A cup of ice
30ml vodka
30ml Kahlua (or any coffee
liqueur)
30ml milk (we use oat)

Step 1
Brew the tea in a Brewdini or tea strainer with the
boiling water for 4 minutes, then strain and whisk
in the hot chocolate powder until it's dissolved.
Leave to cool. This will make a chocolatey chai
concentrate.

Step 2
Once completely cooled, add 50ml of the tea
concentrate to a cocktail shaker with the ice or
pour into a glass of ice.

Step 3
Add the vodka and Kahlua. Add the milk of your
choice (we prefer oat for extra creaminess). If using
a cocktail shaker, shake, then pour over a glass
filled with ice. If using a glass, stir the ingredients
together.

HERBAL

Herbal teas, also known as tisanes, are naturally caffeine-free infusions that do not actually contain the tea leaf plant *Camellia sinensis*. Herbs and spices such as chamomile, lavender, mint and ginger are often used in herbal teas for their holistic benefits. Our soothing range of herbal teas includes Deckchair Dreaming, Enchanted Narnia and Dozy Girl plus we are known for our popular wellness teas (see pages 38 – 41) including Good Calmer Turmeric, Cold Weather Warrior and Lemon & Ginger.

All of these are great hot, without milk, brewed for 4+ minutes with 100 °C water. Our herbal blends are also delicious cold brewed in water or lemonade and taste luscious garnished with mint or sliced fruit. If you're looking for something a bit different for a special celebration, or simply want to make a lovely tasty savoury or sweet treat, this chapter will do the trick! Using our award-winning herbal tea blends, chocolatey and fruity herbal tea infusions, this is your chance to create some magical moments, pick-me-ups and mindfulness moments for yourself and your loved ones.

ENCHANTED DREAMS
HOT CHOCOLATE

Serves 1-2

Float away on a cloud into your dreams with this cosy hot chocolate made with our Enchanted Narnia tea. Inspired by the classic treat – Turkish Delight – this dreamy herbal tea is smooth and full of wonder.

PREP 2 mins | **COOK** 5 mins

250ml milk (any kind)
2 tbsp rose tea (we use our **ENCHANTED NARNIA** blend)
40g 70% dark chocolate, broken into pieces
1 tbsp caster sugar
1 tsp vanilla bean paste
A pinch of sea salt flakes

OPTIONAL TOPPINGS
Whipped cream
Marshmallows
Chocolate shavings

Step 1
Heat the milk in a saucepan until warm, then add the tea. Leave to steep for 4 minutes, then strain and return to the saucepan, discarding the tea.

Step 2
Add the chocolate, sugar, vanilla bean paste and salt to the pan over a medium heat. Simmer for 4 minutes, whisking until the hot chocolate is smooth, thick and creamy.

Step 3
Top with whipped cream, marshmallows, and chocolate shavings, if using.

CHAMOMILE HUMMUS

Fall in love with making hummus with this unique recipe bursting with flavour. Made with our super popular chamomile tea blend, Deckchair Dreaming, it's a delightful vegan accompaniment to pair with your fave raw veg, vegan flatbread or your go-to crisps. You can make this with any chamomile tea.

PREP 10 mins | **NO COOK**

2 tbsp chamomile tea (we use our **DECKCHAIR DREAMING** blend)
85ml boiling water
1 x 400g tin chickpeas, drained
1 small garlic clove
Zest and juice of ½ lemon
3 tbsp tahini
1 tbsp olive oil, plus extra to serve
Salt and freshly ground black pepper

OPTIONAL TOPPINGS
Paprika
Chopped flat-leaf parsley or dill

Step 1
Brew the tea in a Brewdini or tea strainer with the boiling water for 4 minutes, then strain. Pour the tea concentrate into a food processor along with the chickpeas, garlic, lemon zest and juice, tahini and oil.

Step 2
Blitz until smooth and season to taste.

Step 3
To serve, drizzle over some olive oil and sprinkle over some paprika and herbs, if using. This will keep for a couple of days in the fridge.

ETON MESS

This lovely twist on a no-bake classic British dessert
is full of naturally sweet, melt in your mouth goodness.
Use either of our popular herbal chamomile tea blends,
Deckchair Dreaming or Dozy Girl, to make the compote, or use any
other type of chamomile tea. This is a glorious summer staple.

PREP 5 mins + cooling | **COOK** 10 mins

**FOR THE RASPBERRY
AND TEA COMPOTE**
3 tbsp chamomile tea
(we use our **DECKCHAIR
DREAMING** or **DOZY GIRL**
blends)
100ml boiling water
Juice of ½ lemon
200g raspberries
4 tbsp honey

TO SERVE
4 meringue nests (60g)
150g clotted cream
150g raspberries or
quartered and hulled
strawberries

Step 1
Brew the tea in a Brewdini or tea strainer with the
boiling water for 4+ minutes, then strain 50ml of the
liquid into a small saucepan.

Step 2
Add the lemon juice, raspberries and honey to the
pan over a medium heat. While cooking, mash
the raspberries with the back of a spoon. Simmer
for 5–8 minutes until the mixture has thickened
slightly. Set aside to cool completely.

Step 3
Once cool, assemble in 4–6 small ramekins. Crush
the meringue nests and layer them with little
spoonfuls of the clotted cream, raspberries and the
tea compote.

DECKCHAIR DREAMING COCKTAIL

Serves 4

Perfect for the beach or the back garden, this refreshing, minty and calming drink made with our Deckchair Dreaming herbal blend of chamomile, with hints of crisp apple, will have you dreaming all year round. You can also use any herbal tea, such as our Dozy Girl tea.

PREP 5 mins + cooling | **NO COOK**

8 tsp chamomile tea (we use our **DECKCHAIR DREAMING** blend)
900ml boiling water
A handful of ice
3 limes
240ml white rum (optional)
Fresh mint leaves (optional)

Step 1
Brew the tea in a Brewdini or tea strainer with the boiling water for 3 minutes. Strain and place in the fridge to cool. Alternatively, you can put the steeping tea in the fridge overnight using a cold brew tea bottle (see page 28).

Step 2
Once cooled, get your glasses or cocktail shaker and half-fill with the ice.

Step 3
Squeeze the juice of half a lime over the ice. Top up with 50ml of water for a mocktail or 60ml of white rum for a cocktail. Then stir your glass or shake well and pour.

Step 4
To get that extra fresh flavour, take a few mint sprigs and clap them between your hands to release the flavour, then add to each glass. For extra flair and flavour, top with lime wedges.

Tip

This can easily be made as a mocktail to be enjoyed by everyone!

DELIGHTFUL
DREAMS COCKTAIL

Drift away into a relaxing evening with this dreamy, creamy, chocolatey cocktail. Using our Enchanted Narnia blend, you'll be treating yourself to the most delightful nightcap you've ever had. You can use any herbal rose tea but we do recommend Enchanted Narnia.

PREP 5 mins | **NO COOK**

1–2 tsp rose tea (we use our **ENCHANTED NARNIA** blend)
100ml boiling water
A cup of ice
50ml coffee liqueur
1 tsp cocoa powder
50ml oat milk
Vegan whip or whipped cream

Step 1
Brew the tea in a Brewdini or tea strainer with the boiling water for 4 minutes. Once cooled, strain the tea into a cocktail shaker and add the ice. Alternatively, if you don't have a shaker, pour directly into a glass with the ice.

Step 2
Add the coffee liqueur and half the cocoa powder.

Step 3
If using a cocktail shaker, add the oat milk, then shake and pour into a serving glass. If using a glass, top the glass with oat milk, then stir.

Step 4
Garnish with whipped cream or vegan whip.

Tip

To turn this cocktail into a mocktail, replace the coffee liqueur with an additional 50ml of tea concentrate (see page 25).

ENCHANTED
NARNIA BROWNIES

Incredibly moreish chocolate brownies made with our herbal,
chocolate and rose tea, Enchanted Narnia. Dreamy, delicious and
chocolatey, this is sure to become your go-to brownie recipe!

PREP 20–30 mins + chilling | **COOK** 30–45 mins

110g unsalted butter
1 tbsp rose tea (we use
our **ENCHANTED NARNIA**
blend)
50g dark chocolate,
broken into pieces
225g granulated sugar
50g plain flour, sifted
(replace with gluten-free
flour if desired)
1 tsp baking powder
¼ tsp salt

**FOR THE TEA-INFUSED
CHOCOLATE FUDGE
TOPPING**
1 tsp rose tea (we use our
ENCHANTED NARNIA
blend)
100ml evaporated milk
75g granulated sugar
100g white chocolate,
broken into small pieces
40g unsalted butter or
margarine

Step 1
For the topping, combine the tea and evaporated
milk in a saucepan and heat over a low heat until
simmering. Simmer for 10 minutes, then strain
(you should end up with around 75ml of milk).

Step 2
Combine the sugar and the tea-infused evaporated
milk in a heavy saucepan. Place the pan over a
low heat and allow the sugar to dissolve, stirring
frequently.

Step 3
When all the granules of sugar have melted, bring
the mixture to the boil and simmer very gently for
6 minutes – this time without stirring.

continues overleaf

Step 4

Take the pan off the heat, stir in the white chocolate and keep stirring until the chocolate has melted. Stir in the butter. When the mixture has cooled a little, transfer it to a bowl, then cover with clingfilm and chill for a couple of hours.

Step 5

Preheat the oven to 180°C/160°C fan and line a 20cm square tin with baking paper.

Step 6

To make the brownie, melt the butter with the tea and heat for around 15 minutes, then strain into a heatproof mixing bowl.

Step 7

Add the dark chocolate to the bowl and set over a saucepan with a small amount of water over a low heat and melt them together.

Step 8

Remove from the heat and stir in all the remaining ingredients, mixing thoroughly.

Step 9

Spread into the prepared tin. Bake for 35–40 minutes (it will firm up as it cools). Leave to cool in the tin.

Step 10

Finally, spread the chocolate fudge topping over the base. If you'd like, you can add a little extra with edible glitter, candy hearts and rose petals to make it extra special. Enjoy! This will keep in an airtight container for up to 5 days.

VICTORIA SPONGE CAKE

Elevate your Victoria Sponge with this showstopper! Infused with our Enchanted Narnia tea, a herbal tea base with chocolate, rose and floral natural flavouring, this is the ultimate take on a sponge cake. This recipe was inspired by Brewbird Veronika.

PREP 45 mins + cooling | **COOK** 25 mins

250g unsalted butter
250g caster sugar
4 medium eggs
250g self-raising flour
1 tbsp milk (any kind)

FOR THE CRÈME DIPLOMATE
200ml whole milk
2 tbsp rose tea (we use our **ENCHANTED NARNIA** blend)
12g cornflour
30g caster sugar
2 large egg yolks
15g unsalted butter, cubed
200ml double cream
100g icing sugar, plus extra for dusting
½ tsp vanilla bean paste

FOR THE COMPOTE
200g frozen raspberries
75g caster sugar
Juice of 1 lemon

TO SERVE
Edible flowers
Fresh berries

Step 1
Preheat the oven to 180°C/160°C fan and line 2 x 20cm round cake tins with baking paper. Put the butter and sugar into a large bowl and beat with an electric whisk until soft and pale. Gradually whisk in the eggs, one at a time, before folding in the flour and milk until you have a soft sponge mixture.

Step 2
Divide the mixture between the prepared tins and spread so they're level. Bake for 25 minutes until golden and a skewer inserted into the centre comes out clean. Leave to cool in the tins for 5 minutes before removing onto a cooling rack to cool completely.

continues overleaf

Step 3

Meanwhile, make the crème diplomate. Heat the milk in a saucepan until steaming and add the tea, then leave to infuse for 10 minutes. Strain and return to the saucepan, discarding the tea leaves, and put the infused milk over a medium heat until simmering.

Step 4

Put the cornflour, caster sugar and egg yolks into a bowl and whisk until pale. Whisk half of the infused milk into the cornflour mix and then whisk it all back into the milk over a low heat. Continue to whisk for 2 minutes until thickened.

Step 5

Pour into a bowl and whisk in the butter. Cover and set aside to cool.

Step 6

Once cool, whisk the double cream, icing sugar and vanilla bean paste together with an electric whisk until medium peaks form. In two batches, whisk the crème pâtissière into the cream until smooth. Cover and chill in the fridge for 2 hours to firm up.

Step 7

To make the compote, put the raspberries, sugar and lemon juice in a saucepan over a medium heat. Cook for 4–5 minutes until the raspberries have just defrosted, the sugar has dissolved, and a syrup has formed. Leave to cool completely.

Step 8

To assemble, put one sponge layer onto a plate, top with the crème diplomate and a few spoons of the raspberry compote in the middle. Place the other sponge on top. Dust the top with icing sugar and garnish with fresh berries and edible flowers if you have them. Serve with the remaining compote.

FRUITY

Fruit teas, also known as tisanes or fruit infusions, are naturally caffeine free, made with real fruit and are delicious either hot or cold. We are world renowned for having the best fruit teas out there, packed full of flavour and natural goodness, and this chapter showcases some of our most popular fruity tea blends used in the tastiest food and drink creations. What's not to love about a fruity ice lolly, a heavenly milkshake or a zesty, fruit-filled summer drink that'll transform your garden parties into celebration soirées.

Although all of these recipes using fruit teas are absolutely gorgeous, the standout recipe in this chapter has got to be Iced Tea Doughnuts. Yum! Fruit teas lend themselves perfectly to cold brewing, which is great for a sugar-free alternative to squash.

MULLED CIDER

Serves 2

Here's a fun twist on the traditional mulled wine festive drink. Made with our warming winter fruit tea, Mulled Cider, with aromatic winter spices, it is the perfect Christmas party tipple with or without alcohol. You can also use any fruit tea with a strong apple flavour.

PREP 5 mins | **COOK** 5 mins

4 tsp apple-flavoured tea (we use our **MULLED CIDER** blend)
100ml boiling water
1 apple
200ml apple juice
Cinnamon stick
25ml brandy or rum if wanting to make boozy!

Step 1
Brew the tea in a Brewdini or tea strainer with the boiling water for 4 minutes.

Step 2
While your tea is brewing, thinly slice the apple.

Step 3
When the tea has brewed, strain it into a pan and add the apple juice and the cinnamon stick. Put the pan over a low heat, and leave the ingredients to infuse for 5 minutes.

Step 4
Add your shot of alcohol at this point, and take the mixture off the heat. Pour into mugs and sip next to a crackling fire!

STRAWBERRY LEMONADE ICE LOLLIES

These juicy, naturally sweet ice lollies are made
with our bestselling fruit tea blend, Strawberry Lemonade.
A hit for summer celebrations or birthday parties with kids big
and small! You can use any fruit tea you like here.

PREP 5 mins + cooling + freezing | **NO COOK**

6 tsp fruit tea (we use our
STRAWBERRY LEMONADE
blend)
675ml boiling water
Sweetener of your choice,
to taste (we use agave
syrup)

Step 1
Brew the tea in a Brewdini or tea strainer with the
boiling water for 4 minutes. Leave to cool, then chill
in the fridge.

Step 2
Once your tea has cooled, add your chosen
sweetener to taste.

Step 3
Pour the tea evenly into 6 ice lolly moulds and place
in the freezer. You will need to add your lolly sticks
when the tea is nearly set so keep an eye out, then
gently push them into the middle of each lolly.
Leave for a few hours, or overnight, to fully set.

Step 4
To release the lollies, dip the moulds very briefly in
hot water and they will easily slide out.

ICED TEA
DOUGHNUTS

Who wouldn't like a tea-infused glaze to add to their doughnuts?
Made with our Strawberry Lemonade tea, these absolutely gorgeous
goodies will brighten any occasion at any time of the day. YUM.
This recipe was inspired by Brewbird Audrey.

PREP 10–15 mins | **COOK** 12–15 mins

Cooking spray, for greasing
(optional)
75g unsalted butter, plus
extra (optional) for
greasing
3 tsp strawberry-flavoured
tea (we use our
STRAWBERRY LEMONADE
blend)
180ml whole milk
260g plain flour
45g caster sugar

45g light soft brown sugar
2 tsp baking powder
¼ tsp salt
2 medium eggs
1½ tsp vanilla extract

FOR A WATER ICING
TOPPING
1 tsp water
1 tsp vanilla extract
150g icing sugar

FOR A CHOCOLATE
GANACHE TOPPING
80ml double cream
2 tsp strawberry-flavoured
tea
80g dark chocolate,
roughly chopped

GARNISH
Sprinkles, freeze-dried
raspberries, rose petals

method overleaf

Step 1

Preheat the oven to 175°C/155°C fan and coat a 12-hole doughnut pan with cooking spray or butter.

Step 2

In a small pan on the hob, melt the butter with 2 teaspoons of the tea leaves. Once melted, allow the tea to steep in the butter off the heat for 10 minutes. Then heat the milk with the third teaspoon of tea until warm but not boiling. Steep for 10 minutes.

Step 3

Meanwhile, place the flour, caster sugar, brown sugar, baking powder and salt in a large bowl. Stir to combine. Then add the eggs and vanilla extract and stir to combine to a thick batter. Strain the tea-infused butter and milk into the bowl and stir until smooth.

Step 4

Place the batter in a piping bag or freezer bag. Cut off the tip of the freezer bag with scissors. Pipe the batter into the prepared doughnut pan. If your pan only has 6 rings, reserve the remaining batter for a second batch.

Step 5

Bake the doughnuts for 10–12 minutes until just golden. Let them rest in the pan for 3 minutes, then turn out onto a cooling rack.

Step 6

If repeating the process with remaining batter, wipe the moulds with kitchen paper and coat with cooking spray or butter before piping in the remaining batter.

Step 7

While the doughnuts are cooling, make your choice of topping (or both). If making water icing, mix together the water and vanilla extract. Slowly add this mixture to the icing sugar and stir until the icing is a thick, drizzling consistency (you may not need all of it). If making chocolate ganache, steep the tea in the cream for 4 minutes in a pan over a low heat, then strain the cream into a heatproof bowl. Add the chocolate and set the bowl over a pan of gently simmering water. Allow the chocolate to melt in the tea-infused cream and stir until combined.

Step 8

When your doughnuts are cool, dip each one into the icing of your choice. Top with sprinkles, freeze-dried fruit, or petals. Let them sit for about 15 minutes until the frosting has started to firm up, then serve.

Tip

Any leftover ganache can be heated gently in the microwave and used on ice cream!

BELLINI

Made with our Blueberry & Peach fruit tea, this is
a naturally sweet, full-flavoured treat for any occasion.
It's sunshine in a flute with a fruity, passionate twist.

PREP 5 mins + brewing overnight | **NO COOK**

1 tsp fruit tea (we use our
BLUEBERRY & PEACH
blend)
100ml lemonade
A handful of ice
50ml vodka
Slice of orange
Edible glitter

Step 1
Cold brew the tea and lemonade in a cold brew
bottle overnight (see page 28).

Step 2
Add the ice and vodka to a glass. Top up the glass
with the cold brewed liquid. Stir.

Step 3
Add the slice of orange and a spritz of edible glitter
to garnish. Enjoy!

PIÑA COLADA

In holiday mode? This fabulous cocktail made with
our Piña Colada fruit tea is fruity and creamy.
Packed full of coconut, pineapple and lots of pretty
flower petals, this is the perfect holiday refresher.

PREP 5 mins + cooling | **NO COOK**

3 tsp coconut and
  pineapple tea (we use
  our **PIÑA COLADA** blend)
100ml boiling water
100ml pineapple juice
60ml white rum
60ml coconut cream
Juice of 1 lime, plus a slice
  (optional) to garnish
A handful of ice
Pineapple leaf or slice, to
  garnish (optional)

Step 1
Brew the tea in a Brewdini or tea strainer with the
boiling water for 4+ minutes, then strain and leave
to cool.

Step 2
Put the tea into a blender along with the pineapple
juice, rum, coconut cream, lime juice and ice. Blitz
until smooth and pour into a glass.

Step 3
Garnish with a lime or pineapple slice or leaf.

A ROYALLY GOOD MILKSHAKE

Tea in a milkshake? Absolutely! Using our delicious Eton Mess tea, why not whip up a shake fit for royalty? Fruity, creamy and dreamy. You could substitute other fruit teas from our Tea Wall, such as Strawberry Lemonade, or any other fruit tea.

Serves 1

PREP 5 mins + cooling | **NO COOK**

3 tsp strawberry tea (we use our **ETON MESS** blend)
100ml boiling water
2 heaped tbsp vanilla ice cream
50g raspberries
50ml milk (optional, any kind)
½ tsp vanilla extract
A small handful of ice

TO SERVE (OPTIONAL)
Whipping cream
A handful of crushed meringue
Raspberries, halved

Step 1
Brew the tea in a Brewdini or tea strainer with the boiling water for 4+ minutes, then strain and leave to cool.

Step 2
Put the tea into a blender and add the ice cream, raspberries, milk, if using, vanilla extract and ice. Blitz until smooth and creamy. Pour into a glass and top with whipped cream, a sprinkling of meringue and the halved berries to serve.

Serves
1

SUMMER IN THE GARDEN

Get out and about with this gorgeous zesty fruit infusion. A beautiful option for barbecues, dinner parties, sporting events or simply enjoyed with friends in the garden. You can use any fruit tea, including our Strawberry & Pomegranate or Blueberry & Peach.

PREP 5 mins + cooling | **NO** COOK

150ml fruit tea concentrate per serving (see page 25, we use our **SUMMER IN THE GARDEN** blend)
50ml Pimm's per serving
A cup of ice
Orange slice
Cucumber slice
A small bunch of mint
Lemonade

Step 1
Add the tea concentrate, Pimm's, ice, orange slice, cucumber slice and mint to a cocktail shaker. Shake, shake, shake!

Step 2
Pour into a glass and top up with lemonade.

Tip

This recipe scales up perfectly for hosting!

ROOIBOS

This cosy chapter features many of our award-winning, naturally caffeine-free rooibos tea blends. Pronounced 'roy–boss' and otherwise known as Redbush tea or red tea, rooibos is native to South Africa and is the perfect option for those who want to avoid or limit their caffeine intake but still want to have plenty of different flavours to choose from.

Rooibos is very versatile, suits most flavour preferences and tastes great with or without milk. In this chapter, you'll find hearty, sweet and savoury goodies to make, as well as seasonal recipes using some of our most popular rooibos blends such as Gingerbread Chai, Apple Strudel, and Let's Be Having Brew.

ROOIBOS AND PUMPKIN SOUP

This seasonal pumpkin soup made with Rooibos Breakfast Cuppa is the perfect deliciously creamy lunch or light supper menu option. You can also use any other rooibos tea – why not try our Carrot Cake, Gingerbread Chai or Ginger Beer blends?

PREP 10 mins | **COOK** 20 mins

3 tbsp rooibos tea (we use our **ROOIBOS BREAKFAST CUPPA**)
800ml hot vegetable stock
1 pumpkin or squash (about 1.5kg), peeled and cut into 3cm chunks
2 onions, roughly chopped
3 garlic cloves
2.5cm piece of ginger, peeled and roughly chopped
A pinch of chilli flakes
200g crème fraîche

TO SERVE
Crispy fried sage leaves
Chilli flakes
Brown bread and butter

Step 1
Steep the rooibos tea in the vegetable stock for 4–5 minutes, then strain into a large saucepan, discarding the tea.

Step 2
Bring the stock to a simmer over a medium heat and add the pumpkin, onions, garlic, ginger and chilli flakes. Cover and simmer for 18–20 minutes until the squash is soft, then add half the crème fraîche. Blend either with a stick blender or in a machine until smooth; season to taste.

Step 3
Serve with crispy fried sage leaves, chilli flakes, a swirl of the remaining crème fraîche and some brown bread and butter, if you choose.

BANANA BREAD CHAI LOAF

A golden decadent loaf infused with our much loved and ever popular Banana Bread Chai. An aromatic and sensational classic, perfect for breakfast or tea time and you can even stash some away in lunchboxes for later. A beautiful staple.

PREP 25 mins | **COOK** 1 hour 20 mins

200ml whole milk
5 tsp chai (we use our
BANANA BREAD CHAI
blend)
5 mushy bananas (475g
peeled)
125g unsalted butter,
softened, or margarine,
plus extra for greasing
250g caster sugar
1 large egg
1 tsp vanilla extract
300g self-raising flour
½ tsp bicarbonate of soda
150g dark chocolate,
roughly chopped

Step 1
Preheat the oven to 180°C/160°C fan and grease and line a 900g loaf tin with baking paper.

Step 2
Heat the milk in a saucepan over a medium heat and add the chai. Slowly bring to the boil, but don't let it boil. This will take about 6–8 minutes. Keep stirring throughout and the milk should end up a golden brewed colour. Pour the milk through an infuser or sieve to filter out the loose tea leaves, then let the milky tea cool.

Step 3
While the milk is cooling, roughly mash the bananas, making sure to keep them a little chunky.

Step 4
Put the butter and sugar in a bowl and cream together with an electric whisk. Add the egg, vanilla extract, mashed bananas and cooled milk and whisk to combine.

Step 5

Sift half the flour and the bicarbonate of soda into the same bowl and fold into the mixture carefully. Once the mixture is fully mixed, sift in the remaining flour and fold in again. Fold in three-quarters of the dark chocolate chunks.

Step 6

Pour the mixture evenly into the prepared tin and sprinkle with the remaining chocolate. Bake for 1 hour 20 minutes or until a skewer inserted into the centre comes out clean. You may have to cover it with foil three-quarters of the way through if it's turning brown quickly.

Step 7

Leave in the tin to cool completely, then remove and slice to serve. After a few days (if it has lasted that long), your loaf will go a little harder, but then it is great for toasting. Serve with a generous spread of salted butter and a cup of tea. Bliss!
You could even dip it into honey, just like soldiers and boiled eggs.

117

FESTIVAL SPICED RUM CHAI

Serves 2

This is Bird & Blend's most iconic chai, made with our award-winning Gingerbread Chai tea. We've been known to mix this up in a pan and serve it with, or without, rum at festivals. You can also make this using any chai of your choice.

PREP 10 mins | **NO COOK**

50ml spiced rum
2 tsp vanilla syrup
2 tsp cinnamon syrup
200ml rooibos chai tea concentrate (see page 25 – we use our **GINGERBREAD CHAI** blend)
200ml milk (any kind)
Ground cinnamon, for dusting

Step 1
Add the rum (if using) and syrups to a pan and gently stir over a low heat.

Step 2
Add the tea concentrate and milk, and froth.

Step 3
Serve in your chosen mug, garnished with a sprinkle of cinnamon.

Tip
This recipe scales up perfectly for hosting!

118

GINGERBREAD CHAI CAKE

This show-stopping celebration cake is a special treat for chai lovers who want to impress their friends and family. This cake keeps for up to 5 days, but we don't think there'll be any left once you get started on it! This can be made with any chai or rooibos tea.

PREP 20 mins
(+ 30 mins steeping + 1 hour chilling for infused butter)

COOK 20–23 minutes
(+ 5 mins for the infused butter)

250g unsalted butter
4 tbsp chai or rooibos tea (we use our **GINGERBREAD CHAI** blend)
225g caster sugar
2 tsp vanilla extract
1 tsp salt
½ tsp baking powder
225g self-raising flour
2 tsp ground cinnamon
1 tsp ground nutmeg
1 tsp ground cardamom
½ tsp ground black pepper
4 large eggs, at room temperature
50g gingernut biscuits, crushed, to decorate (optional)

FOR THE CARAMEL FILLING
300ml double cream
1 x 397g tin Carnation Caramel

Step 1

You can make the tea-infused butter in advance. In a saucepan add the butter and chai and heat gently, stirring until the butter is melted. Take off the heat and leave to cool for 30 minutes or so – the longer you leave it to infuse, the stronger the chai flavour.

Step 2

The tea-infused butter will have started to solidify on cooling, so gently reheat until it is liquid again. Strain the butter into a mixing bowl. Press the tea leaves with the back of a spoon to extract as much butter as you can and scrape any excess from the bottom of the sieve. Discard the tea leaves. You can now leave the butter to re-solidify in the bowl.

continues overleaf

Step 3

Preheat the oven to 195°C/175°C fan and thoroughly grease and line 2 x 20cm straight-sided cake tins.

Step 4

In a mixing bowl, beat together 225g of the tea-infused butter, the sugar, vanilla extract and salt until light and fluffy; this will take about 5 minutes. Meanwhile, sift the baking powder, flour and spices into a bowl.

Step 5

Add the eggs, one at a time, to the butter and sugar, beating for a minute and adding in a spoonful of the sifted flour mixture if it begins to curdle. Add the remaining flour and spices and briefly whisk to combine. Scrape the bottom of the bowl and beat briefly, to incorporate any residue.

Step 6

Scoop the batter evenly into the prepared tins and smooth out the tops using a small spatula. Bake for 20–23 minutes until golden brown. Remove the cakes from the oven and leave to cool in the tins for 5 minutes before turning them out onto a rack to cool completely.

Step 7

Meanwhile, prepare the filling and topping by whipping the cream and three-quarters of the caramel together until soft peaks hold their shape. Place one sponge onto a plate and spread over two-thirds of the caramel cream. Sandwich the other sponge on top and finish with the remaining caramel cream on top.

Step 8

In a heatproof bowl, heat the remaining caramel in the microwave for 20 seconds. Drizzle over the remaining caramel to serve. Sprinkle over the crushed gingernut biscuits, if using.

APPLE CIDER AND PECAN PUDDING

Perfect for the winter months, using our delicious Apple Strudel tea, this sweet apple-y sponge gives way to a melting puddle of caramel-scented sauce. Serve with a dollop of vanilla ice cream, double cream or custard. This can be made with any rooibos tea.

PREP 20 mins | **COOK** 40 mins

2 medium Bramley or cooking apples, peeled, cored and sliced into 2.5cm-thick wedges
140g self-raising flour
100g golden caster sugar
1 tsp baking powder
A pinch of salt
85g unsalted butter, melted, plus extra for greasing
1 large egg, beaten
1 tsp vanilla extract
Vanilla ice cream or pouring cream, to serve

FOR THE SAUCE
250ml boiling water
1 heaped tbsp apple-flavoured rooibos tea (we use our **APPLE STRUDEL** blend)
120g dark soft brown sugar
75g pecans, roughly chopped

Step 1
Preheat the oven to 180°C/160°C fan. Grease a baking dish with butter. Arrange the apple slices in a layer over the bottom of the dish.

Step 2
Put the flour, caster sugar, baking powder and salt into a bowl. In a separate bowl, mix the melted butter, egg and vanilla extract. In another bowl, whisk this into the dry ingredients until smooth. Pour this over the apple and smooth with a spatula.

Step 3
For the sauce, steep the tea in boiling water in a Brewdini or strainer for 3 minutes, then drain. Pour the tea over the brown sugar in a jug and stir until smooth. Pour this liquid over the batter and apples in the dish, then scatter over the pecans.

Step 4
Bake for 40 minutes or until the pudding has risen and is golden brown. Leave to sit for 4 minutes, then serve with vanilla ice cream or cream.

SPICED HOT TODDY

This warming tea cocktail features our award-winning spiced rooibos Apple Strudel blend. Expect a fruit and spice infusion of apple, cinnamon and vanilla – all those lovely and cosy flavours. Serve hot or cold, with or without alcohol. Why not have two batches on the go at once – one for the adults and one for the kids?

PREP 5 mins | **COOK** 10 mins

100ml rooibos tea concentrate (see page 25 – we use our **APPLE STRUDEL** blend)
200ml apple juice
100ml water
Apple slice
50ml whiskey or rum (optional)

Step 1
Make the tea concentrate, and add it with the apple juice and water to a pan. Heat slowly until it reaches 90°C.

Step 2
Serve up, mixing in your whiskey or rum if using, and garnish with an apple slice.

Tip
This recipe scales up perfectly for hosting!

BIRTHDAY CAKE MILKSHAKE

Serves 1-2

This will make one BIG milkshake for one (oh, go on!) or two smaller glasses. The ultimate treat for anyone with a sweet tooth, this indulgent shake is a celebration in a glass. You can make it boozy with a shot of rum, or enjoy it as is – we love it either way.

PREP 15 mins + cooling

NO COOK

3 tsp vanilla-flavoured rooibos tea (we use our **BIRTHDAY CAKE** blend)
100ml boiling water
50ml spiced rum (if you want to make it boozy)
50ml milk of your choice
1 large scoop of vanilla ice cream (vegan ice cream works super well too)
Squirty cream (if you're feeling luxurious)
Mini marshmallows
Sprinkles

Step 1
Brew the tea in a Brewdini or tea strainer with the boiling water for at least 4 minutes. Strain and leave to cool.

Step 2
If you have a blender, add the tea concentrate, spiced rum (if using), milk and ice cream, then blend until smooth. Alternatively, if you don't have a blender, you can stir all the ingredients together until smooth.

Step 3
Grab your fave glass (big gin glasses work well). Fill it up with the delicious milkshake Garnish with whipped cream, mini marshmallows and sprinkles. Enjoy!

SALMON WITH ROOIBOS

This quick, easy and healthy fish dish uses Let's Be Having Brew! rooibos blended with Sri Lankan black tea and fenugreek. You can substitute any other rooibos teas, including our Moondrop Dreams, Whisktea or Nuts About You blends.

PREP 5 mins | **COOK** 15 mins

750ml rooibos tea concentrate (see page 25 – we use our **LET'S BE HAVING BREW!** blend)
1 orange, sliced
1 tbsp honey
4 skin-on salmon fillets
A pinch of chilli flakes (optional)
Cracked black pepper (optional)

FOR THE DRESSING
½ tsp Dijon mustard
1 tsp apple cider vinegar
1 tsp honey
4 tbsp olive oil

FOR THE SALAD
80g watercress
1 x 250g pouch cooked mixed grains
1 orange, segmented

Step 1
Put the tea concentrate, orange and honey into a large, deep frying pan or saucepan and bring to the boil. Turn down to a low simmer and add the salmon. Poach for 6–8 minutes until cooked through and flaky, turning over halfway so it cooks evenly.

Step 2
Whisk all the dressing ingredients together. Put the watercress, grains and orange into a bowl with the salad dressing and toss to combine.

Step 3
Put the salad on four plates with a salmon fillet on each. Top the salmon with the cooked orange slices and a sprinkling of chilli flakes and cracked black pepper to serve if you like.

MATCHA

Matcha is at the heart of what we do at Bird & Blend: we are the UK's first and largest collection of flavoured matcha green tea powder. In this exciting chapter, we showcase matcha as a versatile ingredient for cooking and baking, in addition to using it to make unique and super tasty drinks. You'll be able to make an eclectic mix of delicious things, including a no-bake matcha cheesecake, matcha protein balls, matcha salad dressing, plus fun party drinks as well. Enjoy discovering the power of matcha tea powder and how it can invigorate your food, sweet treats and bakes!

MATCHA LEMONADE

A zesty, thirst-quenching and revitalising lemonade made with pure grade matcha, or any other matcha – it's tasty, healthy and delicious! Popular at festivals and for those relaxing weekend days after a great night out. Another name for this is the ultimate hangover destroyer!

PREP 10 mins | **NO COOK**

½ tsp pure grade **MATCHA**
100ml water
2 lemon slices, plus a slice to serve
1 tsp lemon syrup
1 tsp honey syrup
A cup of ice
Sparkling water

Step 1
Whisk the matcha and water with a bamboo whisk in a cocktail shaker.

Step 2
Squeeze in the juice of 2 lemon slices, then add the slices, lemon syrup, honey syrup and ice.
Shake, shake, shake!

Step 3
Pour into a cup and top up with sparkling water.
Serve with a slice of lemon on each glass.

BLUEBERRY MATCHA
NO-BAKE CHEESECAKE

Serves 6–8

This no-bake zesty and chocolatey cheesecake is super easy to make and absolutely delicious. Matcha lovers who are looking for something sweet and showstopping, this one's for you!

PREP 20–25 mins
+ 30 mins freeze
and overnight chill

NO COOK

150g digestive biscuits
70g unsalted butter
100g white chocolate, broken into pieces
350g cream cheese
2 tsp caster sugar
2 tsp **LEMON MATCHA**, plus extra for dusting
100g fresh blueberries, roughly chopped, plus extra to decorate

Step 1

Line the base of a 20cm springform cake tin with clingfilm, ensuring there is an overhang of 2–3cm around the edge. Line the sides with a strip of greaseproof paper – this makes sure your cheesecake has nice, smooth edges.

Step 2

Place the biscuits in a sealable plastic bag and lay flat. Push out the air and seal before smashing into small crumbs with a rolling pin. Alternatively, you can blitz the biscuits in a small food processor until fine.

Step 3

Melt the butter in a bowl and add the biscuits – mix well to combine. Pour the biscuit mixture into the prepared tin, pushing it down with a spoon to create an even, compact base. Freeze for 30 minutes.

continues overleaf

Step 4
Meanwhile, melt the white chocolate in a large heatproof bowl. Allow to cool slightly (about 2 minutes) before mixing in the cream cheese and sugar. You can do this with a wooden spoon, but it's great to use an electric whisk to create a light texture. Sprinkle in the matcha and whisk until combined. Finally, stir through the blueberries.

Step 5
Pour the mixture onto the set biscuit base, smooth out the top and put in the fridge overnight.

Step 6
Top with a dusting of matcha powder, and some fresh blueberries.

MATCHA COOKIES

Makes
20

In no time at all, you can whip up a batch of these dreamy chocolate cookies made with our ceremonial grade pure grade matcha. You can substitute any matcha including our Ice Cream, Salted Caramel or Birthday Cake matcha. If you need some fuel to keep you up all night, these cookies are absolutely the answer – and yummy too!

PREP 20 mins   **COOK** 12 mins

125g unsalted butter, softened
275g caster sugar
1 large egg
2 tbsp pure grade **MATCHA**
1 tsp vanilla bean paste
300g plain flour
½ tsp baking powder
2 tbsp water
125g dark chocolate, chopped into chunks
½ tsp sea salt flakes

Step 1
Preheat the oven to 190°C/170°C fan and line two flat baking sheets with baking paper.

Step 2
Whisk the butter and sugar in a large bowl until pale and fluffy. Whisk in the egg until combined.

Step 3
Fold in the matcha, vanilla bean paste, flour and baking powder, and add the water until you have a soft dough. Fold in three-quarters of the chocolate.

Step 4
Divide the dough into 50g balls, roll out and press down to 2cm thick. Press in the remaining chocolate chunks and the sea salt. Transfer the cookies onto the baking sheets, about 4cm apart.

Step 5
Bake for 12 minutes until puffed up slightly and cracked on top. Leave on the trays to cool completely.

MATCHA
PROTEIN BALLS

Recharge with these tasty bite-sized energy balls made with pure grade matcha, great for a pick-me-up at home or a healthy on-the-go boost. You can substitute any of our other matcha flavours, such as Super, Ice Cream or Banana.

PREP 20 mins | **NO COOK**

50g rolled oats
50g desiccated coconut, plus 50g to decorate
1½ tsp pure grade **MATCHA**
30g ground almonds
70g cashew butter
60g honey

Step 1
Put all the ingredients into a small food processor and blitz until you have a stiff but pliable dough.

Step 2
Place the remaining 50g desiccated coconut into a large flat dish. Divide the matcha dough into 25g balls (slightly smaller than a ping pong ball) and then roll in the desiccated coconut until fully covered. These will keep for a couple of days in an airtight container in the fridge.

WHITE CHOCOLATE MATCHA MUFFINS

Using our ceremonial grade pure grade matcha, these sweet little bakes will bring white chocolate and matcha joy to any household. You can substitute any matcha. These are an absolute must – everyone you make them for will love them!

PREP 20 mins   **COOK** 25 mins

320g plain flour
200g caster sugar
1 tbsp pure grade **MATCHA**
A pinch of fine sea salt
2 tsp baking powder
300ml whole milk
180ml vegetable oil
200g white chocolate chips
Icing sugar, for dusting
   (optional)

Step 1
Preheat the oven to 180°C/160°C fan and line a 12-hole muffin tray with paper cases.

Step 2
Sift the flour, sugar, matcha, sea salt and baking powder into a mixing bowl. Stir well to ensure all the ingredients are evenly mixed. Set aside.

Step 3
In a large bowl, thoroughly whisk together the milk and oil. Slowly start adding the dry ingredients to the wet mix until you have a smooth mixture, then fold in the chocolate chips.

Step 4
Fill each muffin case with the batter until they're three-quarters full. Bake for 20–25 minutes, or until the tops are starting to turn golden.

Step 5
Leave in the tray to cool completely before serving. Sprinkle with some icing sugar if you like.

BANANA MATCHA PANCAKES

These naturally sweet, gluten-free pancakes are ready in just 20 minutes. Top with yoghurt, honey, syrup, jam, peanut butter, or any fruit. You can substitute any flavoured matcha, including our Buttermint, Ice Cream or Peaches & Cream blends.

PREP 5 mins | **COOK** 18 mins

2 bananas, 1½ mashed (150g) and ½ sliced
2 medium eggs
1 tsp vanilla bean paste
1 tsp pure grade **MATCHA**
¼ tsp baking powder
A pinch of mixed spice
A small pinch of salt
3 tsp olive oil

TO SERVE
Natural yoghurt
Fresh berries

Step 1
Whisk the mashed bananas with the eggs and vanilla bean paste. Then add the matcha, baking powder, mixed spice and salt.

Step 2
You'll have to cook the pancakes in batches. Put 1 teaspoon of the oil into a large frying pan over a medium heat and, once hot, add 3 tablespoons of the pancake batter, spreading out slightly to form a circle. Fry for 3 minutes on each side, turning over carefully. Remove from the pan and repeat with the remaining oil and batter.

Step 3
Serve with a dollop of yoghurt and berries.

MATCHA
SALAD DRESSING

Makes 200ml

A new way to love your salad! Top with this gorgeous healthy matcha-infused dressing made with pure grade matcha. Why not experiment with flavours by substituting other matcha flavours, such as our Lemon, Raspberry Ripple or Apple & Mint blends?

PREP 15 mins | **NO COOK**

1 tsp pure grade **MATCHA**
60ml rice vinegar
1 tbsp honey
1 tbsp orange juice
120ml sunflower or
   grapeseed oil
1 tsp finely minced
   shallots
Sea salt and ground black
   pepper

Step 1
Vigorously whisk the matcha in the rice vinegar for 1 minute.

Step 2
Whisk in the honey and orange juice, then gradually whisk in the oil.

Step 3
Mix in the shallots and season with sea salt and freshly ground black pepper, to taste.

Step 4
Enjoy over your favourite mixed green salad or steamed greens. This dressing will keep in the fridge for up to a couple of weeks.

MATCHA
BEES KNEES

This easy to make, floral honey cocktail using our mouthwatering Lemon Matcha creates a refreshing cocktail with layers upon layers of flavour. Substituting our pure grade matcha (or any other kind of pure matcha) here works very well for this drink too.

PREP 5 mins | **NO COOK**

½ tsp matcha (we use our
  LEMON MATCHA)
100ml water
2 lemon slices
25ml honey
25ml gin
A glass of ice
Sparkling water
Slice of lemon or fresh
  honeycomb, to garnish
  (optional)

Step 1
Whisk the lemon matcha and water with a bamboo whisk. Add this to a cocktail shaker with the lemon slices, their juice, the honey and gin. Add the ice. Shake, shake, shake!

Step 2
Pour into your chosen glass, top up with sparkling water and garnish with a slice of lemon.

Step 3
To garnish, add a slice of lemon or fresh honeycomb, cut into cubes, if you like.

VAMPIRE'S BLOOD
PARTY DRINK

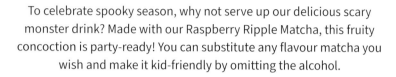

To celebrate spooky season, why not serve up our delicious scary monster drink? Made with our Raspberry Ripple Matcha, this fruity concoction is party-ready! You can substitute any flavour matcha you wish and make it kid-friendly by omitting the alcohol.

PREP 15 mins | **NO COOK**

50g strawberries
A handful of ice
50ml tequila
500ml lemonade
½ tsp raspberry matcha
(we use our **RASPBERRY RIPPLE MATCHA**)
Spooky sweets and
decorations, to garnish

Step 1
Mash the strawberries finely in a bowl, then transfer to two glasses. Add ice to your liking. For a little bit of extra spookiness, you could freeze fake spiders into the ice.

Step 2
Add the tequila. Top up with the lemonade.

Step 3
Whisk the matcha with 150ml cold water, then pour this on top of the cocktail.

Step 4
Add spooky decorations as you please. We added some eyeball sweets on a skewer!

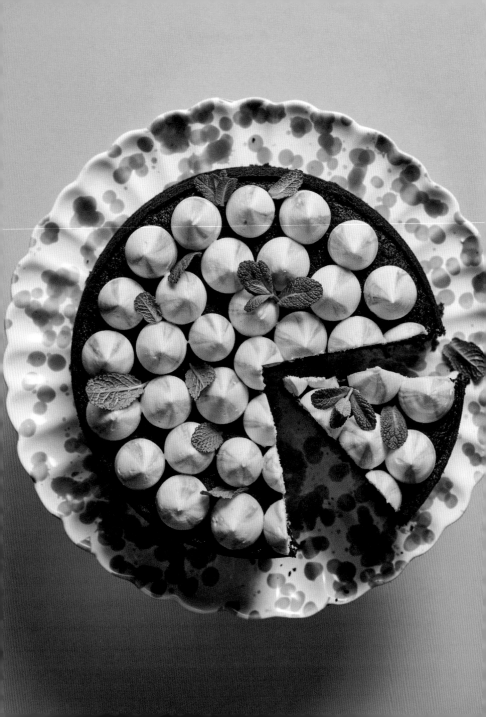

INDEX

Note: page numbers in **bold** refer to recipe illustrations.

A

Ankara Apple 12, 63, 68
apple 12–14, 16, 63, 68
  apple cider and pecan
    pudding **124**, 125
  Mulled Cider 100
  Apple Strudel 16, 113,
    125–6

B

B Corp certification 9
Banana Bread Chai 16
  Banana Bread Chai loaf
    116–17
banana matcha pancakes
  143
Bellini 105
Bird & Blend Tea Co. 6,
  8–9
  Tea Wall 10–17
Birthday Cake 17
  Birthday Cake
    milkshake 127
black tea 24, 44–58
blackcurrant green tea
  spritz 62
Blueberry & Peach 14, 105
blueberry matcha
  no-bake cheesecake
  133–4, **135**
Bottle, Cold Brew 20
breakfast cocktail, the
  best boozy 46, **47**
brewing guide 24
brewing temperature
  21, 27

brownies, Enchanted
  Narnia 93–4

C

caffeine 44
caffeine-free teas 13, 16,
  85, 99, 113
cakes
  autumn spiced caramel
    Bundt cake 57–8, **59**
  Banana Bread Chai loaf
    116–17
  Earl Grey yoghurt loaf
    48–9, **51**
  peppermint and
    chocolate cake **74**,
    75–6, **76–7**
  tea loaf 79
  Victoria sponge cake
    95–6, **97**
  white chocolate matcha
    muffins 142
caramel 11
  autumn spiced caramel
    Bundt cake 57–8, **59**
  caramel filling **120**,
    121–2, **122–3**
cardamom 12, 16, 57–8
cashew butter 140
chamomile 13, 90
  chamomile hummus 88
cheesecake, blueberry
  matcha no-bake 133–4,
  135
chickpeas 88
chilli flavours 12

Chinese Treasures 11,
  66, 70
chocolate 12, 13
  Banana Bread Chai loaf
    116–17
  choccy biccy milk tea
    50, 52
  chocolate ganache **102**,
    103–4
  delightful dreams
    cocktail 92
  Enchanted Narnia
    brownies 93–4
  matcha cookies **136**,
    137, **138–9**
  peppermint and
    chocolate cake **74**,
    75–6, **76–7**
  see also hot chocolate;
    white chocolate
Chocolate Digestives 11,
  35, 45, 52
cinnamon 12, 14, 16, 31,
  34, 56–8, 66, 70, 100,
  118, 121–2
clove 12, 14
cocktails
  Bellini 105
  the best boozy breakfast
    cocktail 46, **47**
  Deckchair Dreaming
    cocktail 90, **91**
  delightful dreams 92
  festival spiced rum chai
    118, **119**
  g & tea 53

green tea gimlet 68, **69**
matcha bees knees **146**, 147
mojitea 67
Mulled Cider 100
oolong white Russian 82, **83**
piña colada **106**, 107
spiced hot toddy 126
Summer in the Garden 110, **111**
vampire's blood party drink 148, **149**
coconut 14
coconut cream 107
coconut (desiccated) 140
coconut milk
hot choco-latte 78
ombre ice lollies 80, **81**
coffee 75–6
coffee liqueur 92
see also Kahlua
cold brew tea 20, 28
see also iced tea
Cold Brew Tea collection 29
Cold Weather Warrior 39, 41, 85
compost 23
compote
raspberry 95–6, **97**
raspberry and tea 89
cookies, matcha **136**, 137, **138–9**
crème diplomate 95–6, **97**

D

Deckchair Dreaming 13, 41, 85, 88–90
Deckchair Dreaming cocktail 90, **91**
delightful dreams cocktail 92

Digester, The, The Digester wellness drink 38
doughnuts, iced tea **102**, 103–4
Dozy Girl 13, 85, 89
dressings 128, 144, **145**

E

Earl Grey Creme 11, 45
Earl Grey Creme latte 33
Earl Grey yoghurt loaf 48–9, **51**
Enchanted Narnia 13, 85–6, 92
crème diplomate 95–6, **97**
Enchanted Narnia brownies 93–4
equipment 20–4
Eton Mess (blend) 108
Eton mess (recipe) 89

F

fruity teas (tisanes) 24, 98–110

G

g & tea 53
ganache, chocolate **102**, 103–4
gimlet, green tea 68, **69**
gin-based cocktails 46, **47**, 53, 147
ginger 14, 17, 34, 40–1, 66
ingwer tea 41
Gingerbread Chai 17, 34, 113–14, 118
Gingerbread Chai cake **120**, 121–2, **122–3**
green tea 12, 21, 23
blackcurrant green tea spritz 62

brewing guide 24
green tea gimlet 68, **69**
green tea latte 66
green tea miso soup 62, **64–5**
green tea poached pears 70, **71**
how to 26–7
recipes 60–70

H

herbal teas (tisanes) 24, 84–96
hot chocolate
chocolate indulgent latte 35
enchanted dreams hot chocolate 86, **87**
hot choco-latte 78
hot lattes 25
hot toddy, spiced 126
hummus, chamomile 88

I

Ice Cream Matcha 37
ice lollies
ombre 80, **81**
Strawberry Lemonade 101
iced tea
classic iced tea 29
how to 28
iced chai 31
iced tea doughnuts **102**, 103–4
iced tea latte 25
iced tea with lemonade 25
iced vanilla matcha latte 36
mojitea 67
Moondrop Dreams iced latte 32

icing 75–6
  water **102**, 103–4
immunity warrior 39
infusers 21, 22–3
ingwer tea 41

K

Kahlua 82

L

lattes
  the best chai latte 34
  chocolate indulgent
    latte 35
  Earl Grey Creme latte
    33
  green tea latte 66
  hot choco-latte 78
  hot lattes 25
  iced tea latte 25
  iced vanilla matcha
    latte 36
  Moondrop Dreams iced
    latte 32
  the perfect matcha
    latte 37
  the ultimate pumpkin
    spiced latte 56
lavender flavours 13, 32
lemon 14, 15, 39, 70, 75–6,
  79, 88, 89, 132
  matcha bees knees **146**,
    147
  Strawberry Lemonade
    iced tea 30
Lemon & Ginger 40–1, 85
Lemon Matcha 15, 133,
  147
lemonade 13, 20, 85
  Bellini 105
  blackcurrant green tea
    spritz 62
  classic iced tea 29

g & tea 53
iced tea with lemonade
  25
matcha lemonade 132
Summer in the Garden
  110
vampire's blood party
  drink 148
see also Strawberry
  Lemonade
Let's Be Having Brew! 16,
  113, 128
lime 12, 67, 68, 90
loose leaf tea 21, 22–3

M

matcha 15, 20
  banana matcha
    pancakes 143
  blueberry matcha
    no-bake cheesecake
    133–4, **135**
  iced vanilla matcha
    latte 36
  Lemon Matcha 15, 133,
    147
  matcha bees knees **146**,
    147
  matcha cookies **136**,
    137, **138–9**
  matcha lemonade 132
  matcha protein balls
    140, **141**
  matcha salad dressing
    144, **145**
  the perfect matcha
    latte 37
  Pure Grade Matcha 15,
    36, 132, 137, 140,
    142–4, 147
  Raspberry Ripple
    Matcha 148
  recipes 130–48

white chocolate matcha
  muffins 142
Matcha Milk Frother 21
meringue, Eton mess 89
milk frothers 21
Milk Oolong Chai 12,
  79–80, 82
milkshakes
  Birthday Cake 127
  a royally good 108,
    109
mint 39, 67, 90
  see also Peppermint
    Cream
miso, green tea miso soup
  62, **64–5**
MojiTEA 12, 63
  mojitea cocktail 67
Moondrop Dreams,
  Moondrop Dreams iced
  latte 32
muffins, white chocolate
  matcha 142
Mulled Cider 14
  Mulled Cider cocktail
    100

N

nutmeg 56, 66, 121–2

O

oats 140
ombre ice lollies 80, **81**
oolong 11–12, 72–82
  brewing guide 24
  oolong white Russian
    82, **83**
orange 46, 128, 144

P

pancakes, banana matcha
  143
peach flavours 14

pear, green tea poached
70, **71**
pecan and apple cider
pudding **124**, 125
peppermint and
chocolate cake **74**,
75–6, **76–7**
Peppermint Cream 12,
78
peppermint and
chocolate cake **74**,
75–6, **76–7**
Pimm's 110
Piña Colada 14
Piña Colada cocktail
106, 107
pomegranate flavours 12
protein balls, matcha
140, **141**
pudding, apple cider and
pecan **124**, 125
pumpkin
rooibos and pumpkin
soup 114, **115**
the ultimate pumpkin
spiced latte 56

R

raspberry
raspberry compote
95–6, **97**
raspberry and tea
compote 89
a royally good
milkshake 108, **109**
Raspberry Ripple Matcha
148
rooibos 16, 17, 112–28
brewing guide 24
rooibos and pumpkin
soup 114, **115**
Rooibos Breakfast Cuppa
114

rose flavours 13, 85–6,
92–6
rum-based cocktails 67,
90, 100, 107, 126–7
festival spiced rum chai
118, **119**

S

salad dressing, matcha
144, **145**
salads 128
salmon with rooibos 128,
129
Smoky Russian 11, 45–6
smoky tea steak 54, **55**
sore throat soother 40
soup
green tea miso 62, **64–5**
rooibos and pumpkin
114, **115**
Spiced Pumpkin Pie 56–8
spritzes, blackcurrant
green tea 62
steak, smoky tea 54, **55**
Steepers, Brewdini
Gravity 20, 24
strawberry, vampire's
blood party drink 148,
149
Strawberry Lemonade 14,
30, 103–4
Strawberry Lemonade
ice lollies 101
Strawberry Lemonade
iced tea 30
Summer in the Garden,
Summer in the Garden
cocktail 110, **111**
sustainability 8–9

T

tahini 88
tea concentrate 25

tea leaves, waste 23
tea loaf 79
Tea Tasting Club 9
teapots 22–3
tequila-based drinks 148,
149
Toffee Chai 31
tofu, green tea miso soup
62, **64–5**

V

vampire's blood party
drink 148, **149**
vanilla 11, 16
iced vanilla matcha
latte 36
Victoria sponge cake
95–6, **97**
vodka 82, 105
green tea infused 68

W

waste 23
wellness teas 38–41
Whisk, Bamboo Matcha
20
whiskey-based cocktails
126
white chocolate
blueberry matcha
no-bake cheesecake
133–4, **135**
white chocolate matcha
muffins 142
white Russian, oolong
82, **83**
white tea 24

Y

yoghurt 57–8, 75–6
Earl Grey yoghurt loaf
48–9, **51**

This book is for all of our Teabirds past, present and future who love our tea and have supported and inspired us right from the start. It is for tea lovers, eco warriors, and people who love to be creative in the kitchen. Thank you all for purchasing our book and helping us to spread happiness and reimagine tea! And thank you for supporting our mission to place people and planet at the heart of everything we do while using our company as a force for good.

I'd like to also thank my Brand team, who are as passionate about Bird & Blend as I am, and who have dedicated lots of time, energy and creativity to the success of this book, fuelled by so many delicious cups of tea of course! A special shout out to Rosie, who is our much loved in-house graphic designer, and the talent behind our beautiful visual branding.

Krisi x

Visit our website
here:

Ebury Press, an imprint of Ebury Publishing
20 Vauxhall Bridge Road
London SW1V 2SA

Ebury Press is part of the Penguin Random House group of companies
whose addresses can be found at global.penguinrandomhouse.com

Text © Ebury Press 2024
Design © Ebury Press 2024
Photography © Ebury Press 2024

Illustrations © Bird & Blend Tea Co. 2024 (by Rosie Fairfolm)

Bird & Blend Tea Co. has asserted its right to be identified as the author
of this Work in accordance with the Copyright, Designs and Patents Act 1988

Additional recipe credits: Audrey Bufalini (page 103); Maddy Kimberley/
@sailorandscout (page 57); Veronika (page 95)

First published by Ebury Press in 2024

www.penguin.co.uk

A CIP catalogue record for this book is available from the British Library

Project Editor: Izzy Frost
Publishing Director: Elizabeth Bond
Design: maru studio G.K.
Photography: Haarala Hamilton
Food Stylists: Holly Cochrane and Lucy Turnbull
Prop Stylist: Daisy Shayler-Webb

Printed and bound in Great Britain by Bell and Bain Ltd, Glasgow

ISBN 9781529937398

The authorised representative in the EEA is Penguin Random House Ireland,
Morrison Chambers, 32 Nassau Street, Dublin D02 YH68.

MIX
Paper from
responsible sources
FSC® C018179
www.fsc.org